TAXATION AND THE INCENTIVE TO WORK

A report prepared for the Commission of the European Communities, Directorate-General for Employment and Social Affairs

BY

C. V. BROWN

OXFORD UNIVERITY PRESS

1980

Oxford University Press, Walton Street, Oxford OX2 6DP
London Glasgow New York Toronto
Delhi Bombay Calcutta Madras Karachi
Kuala Lumpur Singapore Hong Kong Tokyo
Nairobi Dar Es Salaam Cape Town
Melbourne Wellington

and associate companies in
Beirut Berlin Ibadan Mexico City

Published in the United States
by Oxford University Press, New York

© ECSC, EEC, EAFC, Brussels—Luxembourg 1980
A document of the Commission of the European
Communities, Directorate—General for Scientific
and Technical Information and Information
Management, Luxembourg

British Library Cataloging in Publication Data
Brown, Charles Victor
    Taxation and the incentive to work.
    1. Incentives in industry
    2. Taxation
    I. Title   II. Commission of the European
Communities. Directorate-General for Scientific
and Technical Information and Information Management.
301.5′5   HF5549.5.15   80-41050
ISBN 0-19-877134-7
ISBN 0-19-877135-5 Pbk

Set by Hope Services, Abingdon
and printed in Great Britain by
Billing & Sons Ltd., Guildford,
London, Oxford and Worcester

PREFACE

The study of the effects of the tax/transfer system on the supply of labour is an obviously important subject in its own right. To take only one example, in the 1979 Budget Speech the British Chancellor of the Exchequer described the income tax cuts designed to increase incentives as the 'keystone' of the government economic strategy. In addition to its intrinsic importance the study of the effects of taxation on labour supply is important as a case study in the application of economic theory. There can be few, if any, parts of micro-economic theory that have been subjected to such widespread and rigorous testing using a variety of methodologies, including the rare (for the social sciences) experimental methodology. The purpose of this book is to provide a relatively non-technical introduction to the subject: to explain the difficulties that have been encountered in applying the simple model of labour supply; to outline the developments in economic theory and econometric technique which have taken place; to present a selection of the labour supply estimates that have been made; and to explain why it is difficult to draw policy implications from these findings.

It should be stressed that the subject of this book is the effects of taxation on the supply of labour and not the effects of taxation on society's welfare. It is important to remember that an increase (decrease) in labour supply could make people worse off (better off) as well as the other way round. The most important reason for the difference is that leisure is generally considered to be a good. If people work more one effect is that they become worse off by reducing their leisure. This subject is extensively discussed in the public finance literature (for example, in Brown and Jackson (1978)).

In this survey no attempt has been made to refer to all the vast literature on the subject. To do so would have detracted from the purpose of the book, but it should be stressed that the absence of a reference to any particular work is in no way intended to imply a derogatory view of the work.

I am grateful to Martin Robertson, who have agreed to the inclusion of certain material from Brown and Jackson (1978) in the present volume.

Extracts from this report were presented as a paper to the Colston Symposium on 'Income Distribution: the Limits to Redistribution', held at Bristol University in the spring of 1979 and will be published in the conference volume. Part of Chapter 9 is based on 'The Effect of the 1979 UK Income Tax Changes on Male Work Incentives. An Approximation', University of Stirling discussion paper, no. 79, by D. J. Sanderson and myself.

I am grateful to members of the Commission staff; to a number of people who have commented on parts of the report, including P. G. Hare, K. Glaister, P. M. Jackson, J. Le Grande, R. J. Ruffell, D. J. Sanderson, and D. T. Ulph; to Mrs C. McIntosh for typing the manuscript and to Mrs S. Hewitt for drawing the diagrams and preparing the index. I accept responsibility for the remaining errors.

This book was originally written as a report to the Commission of the European Communities, where it was financed as part of the programme of Research and Actions on the Development of the Labour Market. In sponsoring its publication in its present form the Commission hopes that the material in it will become more readily available to undergraduates and members of the general public. The analyses and the results presented do not necessarily reflect the views of the Commission, nor do they commit it to a particular view on the labour market or on other policy matters.

C. V. B.
University of Stirling
September 1979

CONTENTS

INTRODUCTION: THE ELEMENTARY THEORY
OF INDIVIDUAL LABOUR SUPPLY

The theory of the labour supply of the individual is an application of basic price theory in which individuals are assumed to try to maximize their satisfaction subject to their budget constraint.

The Basic Theory of Individual Labour Supply

The basic theory of labour supply will be familiar to readers of intermediate economics textbooks. It is assumed that individuals are faced with a choice between a composite consumption good (represented by net income) and leisure. The individuals have an endowment of non-employment income, say rental income or welfare benefits which are *independent* of earnings as well as an endowment of time—say 168 hours a week, and the individual also faces a given wage rate. The consumption possibilities open to the individual can then be represented by a budget constraint such as ABC in Fig. 1.1. In this figure, income is measured on the vertical axis and leisure on the horizontal axis. The initial endowment of time is represented by the horizontal distance OA and non-employment income is represented by the vertical distance AB. The slope of segment BC is determined by the extra net income that can be exchanged for giving up an hour of leisure. This is the net wage rate w. The individual is also assumed to have a given set of preferences between income and leisure which can be represented by a set of well-behaved indifference curves. The individual is said to be in equilibrium when his budget constraint is tangential to the highest attainable indifference curve. Thus in Fig. 1 equilibrium occurs at E, the point of tangency between II and CB. It may be noted that in equilibrium the individual consumes OH hours of leisure and works AH hours.

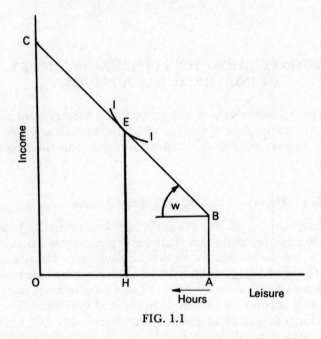

FIG. 1.1

Taxation and the Incentive to Work in the Basic Model

Even within the confines of the basic model different types of taxes will be expected to have rather different sorts of effects on the incentive to work.

Head Taxes (Poll Taxes)

If a flat tax of $X per person is levied the individual will have a reduced set of consumption possibilities. However such a head tax will not affect the return to working more or less. In Fig. 1.2 the tax is given by the distance BB' and $B'C'$ is parallel to BC. Provided that income and leisure are both normal goods the individual will wish, after tax, to consume less of both net income and of leisure, that is to say E_1 will lie to the left of E_0 which means the individual will increase his hours of work from AH_0 to AH_1. This is the familiar case of a pure income effect and because the wage rate represents both the marginal rate of substitution and the marginal rate of transformation there are no distorting effects from the

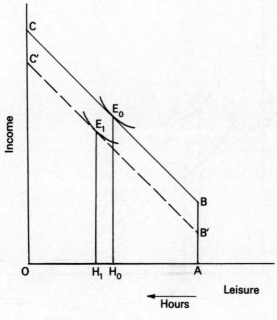

FIG. 1.2

tax. Head taxes are of course a purely regressive tax as the
tax liability of the rich is no greater than that of the poor. It
has been argued, for example by Tinbergen (1977), that to
preserve the advantages of zero marginal tax rates lump-sum
tax rates should be universally adopted. Tax liability would
depend on innate ability measured through a battery of tests.
Most people believe that the practical difficulties in imple-
menting this type of proposal are insurmountable and recognize that a positive marginal rate of tax is necessary.

Proportional Taxes

The simplest example of a positive marginal rate of tax is a
proportional tax (where the marginal and average rates are
equal). The effects of a proportional tax on labour supply
are illustrated in Fig. 1.3 where for convenience non-employment income is assumed to be zero. Pre-tax, the budget
constraint is AB and the individual is in equilibrium at E_0

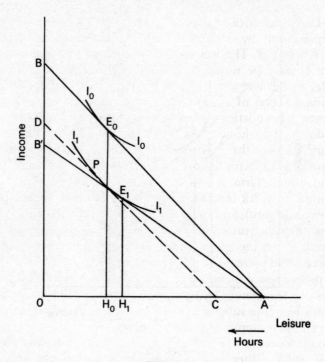

FIG. 1.3

where he works AH_0 hours. A proportional tax at rate t is then introduced which causes the budget constraint to swing down to AB (note that in constrast to Fig. 1.2 there is no change in the budget constraint at zero hours of work). A new equilibrium is reached at E_1. I will refer to this effect as the price effect (it is sometimes called the uncompensated wage effect) by which I mean the effect of a change in the net wage rate leaving the intercept unaffected. The locus of such points corresponds directly to the supply curve of labour. As the diagram is drawn E_1 lies to the right of E_0 which would mean that the tax would reduce work from AH_0 to AH_1 hours. However, this is not a necessary result. To see this we subdivide the movement from E_0 to E_1 into two effects. A proportional tax reduces taxpayers' take-home pay and this will induce people to work longer hours to attempt to maintain their living standards. This first effect, termed the income effect, is very much like a poll tax in its operation. Diagrammatically, like a poll tax, the income effect can be represented by a parallel shift in the budget constraint from AB to CD. The movement from E_0 to P is the income effect. It may be noted that CD was constructed not only parallel to AB but also tangent to I_1I_1, which means that the individual's level of satisfaction is the same at P as it is at E_1. However, a proportional tax changes the net wage rate as well as reducing take-home pay. The reduction in the net wage rate means that the individual will receive a smaller reward for working an extra hour (giving up an hour of leisure). This second effect, termed the substitution effect, will cause an individual to work less (that is, he will substitute the relatively cheaper leisure), and thus move from P to E_1. As Fig. 1.3 is drawn, the substitution effect dominates and labour supply is reduced. If the income effect dominated the introduction of the tax would increase labour supply.

A proportional income tax thus causes an individual both to wish to work more (the income effect) and simultaneously to work less (the substitution effect). At its most basic this is the reason for empirical research on the labour supply effects of taxes. Because our theory tells us that taxes may make people work either less or more the question can only be resolved by empirical research.

Problems of Empirical Research

There are a variety of problems that arise in attempting empirical work in this area and which are discussed in later parts of this work. The elementary theory just outlined assumes that everyone is paid a constant net marginal wage rate. In practice there are a variety of reasons why this may not be so; for example, due to the presence of progressive income taxes. Chapter 2 shows how the theory requires modification to take account of the resulting non-linearities in the budget constraint and also explains some of the resulting econometric difficulties. Chapter 3 contains an account of the problems that arise when attempts are made to measure the variables suggested by the theory. Chapters 4 to 6 contain results from empirical studies of the effects of income taxation on the work-effort of men, applying the individual models of labour supply outlined in Chapters 1 and 2. No attempt is made to discuss all the studies which have been done. Rather than seeking completeness in this sense I have tried to select studies which make clear the main methodological approaches that have been used. In Chapter 4 the results from the interview approach are considered. In Chapter 5 results from cross-section econometric work are given and in Chapter 6 the results from the income maintenance experiments are considered. Chapter 7 contains a discussion of the problems involved in estimating women's labour supply.

The first seven chapters are thus concerned with the individual model of labour supply and its application. The individual model may, however, be inappropriate where labour supply decisions are taken in a household context. The theory and evidence for household models is considered in Chapter 8. Chapter 9 summarizes the empirical evidence and considers the difficulties in drawing policy implications from the labour supply estimates.

2

NON-LINEARITIES IN THE BUDGET CONSTRAINT

In the elementary theory of labour supply outlined in the previous chapter it was assumed that the net marginal wage rate is the same for every hour worked. There are a number of reasons why in practice different hours may be paid at different rates; for example, if some hours are paid at an overtime rate the budget constraint will have two segments (assuming non-employment income is zero). Thus in Fig. 2.1

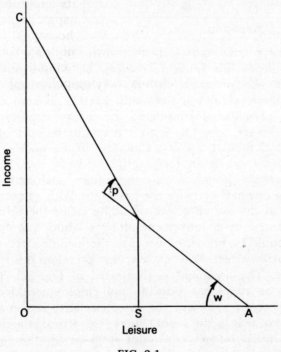

FIG. 2.1

if the standard working week is AS hours and the overtime premium is p then the budget constraint will be ABC where the slope of AB = w and BC = wp. Non-linear budget constraints give rise to two rather different classes of problems.

Perhaps most obviously, the theory itself requires modification to take the non-linearities into account.

The second problem, which arises when one tries to apply the theory, is that when the budget constraint is non-linear it can no longer be argued that the budget constraint is exogenous as is assumed in the theory. The purpose of the present chapter is to explore these two issues.

Labour Supply Theory with Non-Linear Budget Constraints

There are a wide variety of reasons why budget constraints may be non-linear.

Overtime premiums

Overtime premiums have been mentioned, and the complications from this single factor can be considerable if for example the premium differs between overtime worked during the week and at weekends. Even if, as here, only one rate of premium is considered the theory requires modification. To see why this is so it is instructive to look at the theoretical predictions of an increase in the wage rate. Suppose that there is an increase in the basic wage rate with the overtime premium rate remaining unaltered at, say, one and one-half or twice the basic rate. With a linear budget constraint the overall effect would be called the price effect (represented by a movement along a labour supply curve) which could be broken down into the income effect and the substitution effect. With an overtime premium this is no longer true. The argument is illustrated in Fig. 2.2. To keep matters as simple as possible non-employment income is assumed to be zero and the price elasticity is also assumed to be zero, that is, the supply curve is a vertical straight line.[1]

The initial budget constraint is given by the solid line ABC. The individual is in equilibrium at E_0 on the supply curve S_0, which, by assumption, is inelastic. It is critical to the argument to note that the individual would also be at

---

[1] In both cases the argument can be easily modified to allow for these additional complications.

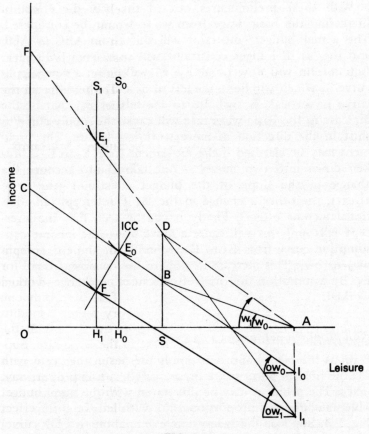

FIG. 2.2

E_0 if the budget constraint were I_0BC rather than ABC. Thus if the individual faced a debt of AI_0 per period and a wage rate of ow_0 his equilibrium would be at E_0. I_0 is thus a hypothetical intercept brought about by the presence of the overtime premium. The higher the overtime premium the larger this 'as if' debt will be. It may seem counter-intuitive to assert that an overtime premium will have an effect akin to a debt. However it must be remembered that a precondition of the overtime premium is that one must work more than AS hours. It would thus be possible to think of the worker as working off the debt during the first AS hours.

With these preliminaries out of the way the effect of increasing the basic wage from w_0 to w_1 can be considered. The actual budget constraint will shift from ABC to ADF and the 'as if' budget constraint will shift from I_0C to I_1F. Equilibrium will now be at E_1. E_1 will be on a new supply curve S_1 which will lie to the left of S_0 and, where the supply curve is vertical, E_1 will lie to the left of E_0, that is, the increase in the basic wage rate will cause the supply curve to shift in the direction of more work/less leisure. This argument may be clarified if the movement from E_0 to E_1 is broken down into two moves — one taking into account the change in the slope of the budget constraint (the price effect), the other a change in the 'as if' intercept (an additional income effect). Firstly it can be seen that the intercept falls and this will cause a move down the income consumption curve from E_0 to F. Secondly the slope rises from ow_0 to ow_1. This increase in slope causes a move from F to E_1. By assumption this price effect causes no change in hours worked.

Non-proportional taxes

Perhaps the most important non-linearities in the tax system for the present purpose are those caused by non-proportional taxes. The problem may be illustrated with the simplest possible example of a proportional tax with an exemption as in Fig. 2.3. Suppose the tax system exempts the first OX_0 units of income and taxes the remainder of units at the rate t. The budget constraint will be ABC with equilibrium at E_0. Suppose a decision is made to cut taxes. This might be achieved either by *increasing* the exemption level or by *reducing* the tax rate and the predicted labour supply effects would be rather different. If the exemption level were raised from OX_0 to OX_1 the actual budget constraint would change from ABC to ADF and the linearized budget constraint would shift from I_0C to I_1F. The new equilibrium would be at E_1 which is assumed to lie on the segment of DF. It is evident that this is a pure income effect involving a movement along the ICC curve and shifting the labour supply curve in the direction of more leisure/less work.

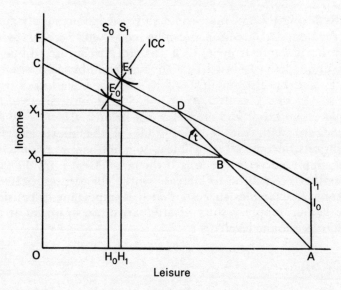

FIG. 2.3

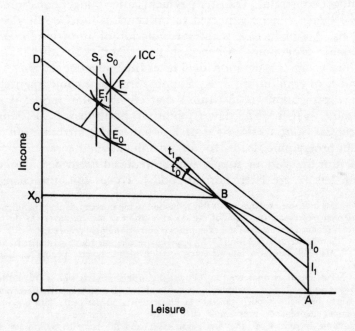

FIG. 2.4

Reducing the tax rate would shift the labour supply curve in the opposite direction as can be seen from Fig. 2.4. Reducing the tax rate from t_0 to t_1 changes the linearized budget constraint from I_0C to I_1D.[2] The new equilibrium position is at E_1 and once again this can be broken down into a price effect (E_0 to F) resulting from the change in the slope of the budget constraint and an additional income effect (F to E_1) associated with the reduced value of the allowance. The additional income effect will lead to additional work, shifting the supply curve to the left. If the price effect is nil then the overall effect will be to increase work. The contrast between these two examples suggests that it is important to consider the labour supply results of alternative tax strategies at the macro-economic level.[3]

Transfers

Transfer payments are another cause of non-linearities in the budget constraint. Transfer payments alter budget constraints and hence can be expected to influence labour supply decisions. A simple case is the introduction of an income maintenance programme[4] when there is no liability to other taxes. Thus in Fig. 2.5 the individual faces the budget constraint AB and is in equilibrium at E_0. Suppose that an income maintenance programme is instituted that changes the budget constraint to ICB.[5] The new equilibrium position is E_1. E_1 must necessarily lie to the right of E_0, that is, the introduction of the programme leads to an unambiguous theoretical prediction that labour supply will be reduced (provided income and leisure are both normal goods). To see this, the change

[2] An intuitive explanation of this reduction in the intercept is that the original intercept represents the value of the tax exemption to the tax payer. As the tax rate is reduced the value of the exemption is correspondingly reduced.

[3] See Brown and Jackson (1978), appendix to Chapter 13.

[4] Also called negative income taxes, social dividends, reverse income taxation, etc.

[5] This might be presented as follows: the official poverty line is OP and the government will raise minimum income level to AI which is half the official poverty line. The implicit tax rate as illustrated is 50 per cent. With a simple income maintenance programme such as the one illustrated any two of the minimum income level, the break-even level, and the tax rate determines the third.

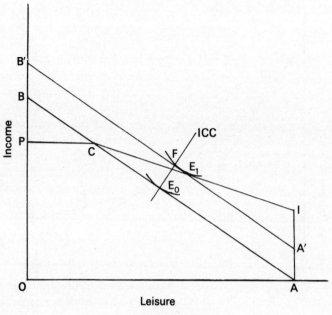

FIG. 2.5

from E_0 to E_1 can be decomposed into two changes. By constructing the line $A'B'$ parallel to AB and tangent to the new higher indifference curve it can be seen that there is an income effect, the movement from E_0 to F along the ICC, that reduces work. There is also a substitution effect, the movement from F to E_1, which also reduces work. Thus the sum of the two effects must reduce work in this case.

This clear prediction depends on the assumption that the budget constraint is linear prior to the introduction of the tax. However this may not be the case, as may be illustrated with reference to Fig. 2.6. Suppose that given existing wages, taxes, and social security benefits the budget constraint ABCD is faced by a group of individuals. If an income maintenance scheme is then introduced, in part to tidy up what might be seen as a confusing morass of benefits, the new budget constraint might look like EFD.

For an individual at E_1 the prediction would be as before: both income and substitution effects reduce work. The opposite would hold for someone at E_3 where both an

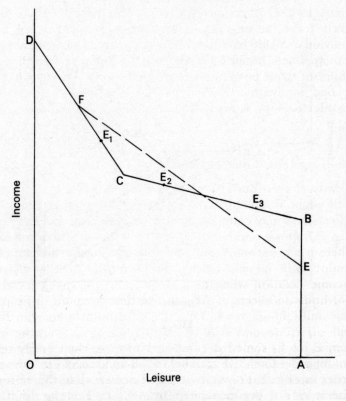

FIG. 2.6

income effect and a substitution effect would increase work. At E_2 no clear *a priori* prediction is possible.

Moonlighting

The presence of second jobs or moonlighting may also cause non-linearities in the budget constraint. Theoretically this case is slightly awkward because it does not make sense for all three of the following assumptions to be satisfied simultaneously: (1) people have two jobs with differing wage rates; (2) they are free to choose their hours in both jobs; and (3) they are indifferent between the two jobs. If (2) and (3) hold, the utility-maximizing individual would choose the job with the higher net wage rate and would work zero hours in the other job. Thus if people have two jobs it is likely to be the case that either (2) or (3) does not hold. An individual might have a second job with a higher new wage rate (perhaps because of tax evasion) but with only limited hours of work possible. Alternatively someone might have a second job with a lower net wage rate because they were unable to work as many hours as they wished in their main job.

Multi-segmented Budget Constraints

Clearly the various factors discussed individually above may well occur in combination. Budget constraints in these circumstances may contain a number of segments. For example, Fig. 2.7 shows one fairly typical pattern for British workers. There is a gross wage (gw) which determines the budget constraint until income reaches the exemption level (OX) for income taxation when tax (at the rate t) becomes payable. For hours in excess of AH_1 an overtime premium (p) is payable until hours reach AH_2, the maximum hours the firm will offer. Beyond AH_2 hours, work is only available in a second job at some lower wage rate (w_{2_0}). There is of course no logical reason why these segments should occur in the order indicated. For example someone with a low gross wage rate may not begin to be liable for income tax until they begin to work overtime.

Comparative static predictions often increase in their complexity as budget constraints become more complex but for someone in equilibrium on the segment DE this may not be the case. For example a change in any of the following would have a pure income effect: gw, t, p, provided that the individual remained on the segment DE and that he evades tax on his second job. An increase in the second job wage rate would cause the supply curve to shift in the direction of more work as can be verified from the diagram (which is drawn on the assumption that price elasticity is zero).

Kinks in Budget Constraints

Budget constraints may of course be more complex than that

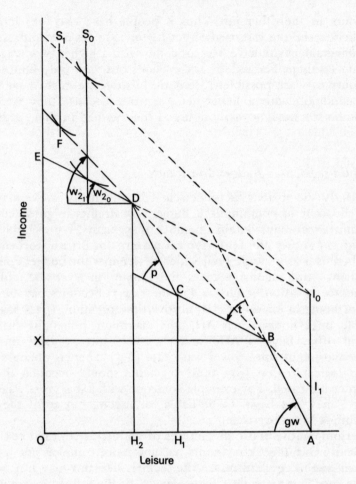

FIG. 2.7

illustrated in Fig. 2.7 if there is more than one tax band or if there are means-tested benefits. With multi-segment budget constraints there is the possibility of 'equilibrium' occurring on one of the concave kinks such as B or D in Fig. 2.7 (A satisfaction-maximizing individual would only be at a convex kink such as C if he were unable to chooose his hours of work). At concave kinks the slope of the budget constraint is not defined and equilibrium might be unaffected by quite substantial changes in the slope of the budget constraint.

Thus an individual working to the point where tax starts (that is, who is at B) could be unaffected by quite substantial changes in tax rate.[6]

While changes in the slope of a budget constraint may sometimes have no effect on behaviour when an individual is at a kink, changes in the position of the kink may be important. The argument may be illustrated by Fig. 2.8. The individual is in 'equilibrium' at E_0 on the budget constraint ABC where he works until his income reaches the tax threshold. If the tax rate is reduced so that his budget constraint becomes ABD, his behaviour is unaffected.[7] However if the tax threshold (the exemption level) were increased from OX_0 to OX_1 the budget constraint would become AFG and the individual would increase his hours of work up to the amount determined by the new threshold, that is, from AH_0 to AH_1. We thus need to note that the predicted effects of an increase in the threshold are not always the same. Someone in equilibrium on BC who moves to a new equilibrium on FG will *decrease* work, while we have seen that someone on the kink will *increase* work.[8] This means that even if all individuals have the same preferences an increase in allowances will cause some to work less, others more.

Econometric Problems of Non-Linear Budget Constraints

The presence of non-linear budget constraints gives rise to serious problems when one attempts to undertake empirical work. Our theory is based on the assumption that people maximize their utility subject to an exogenous budget constraint. There are two problems which arise in econometric work that call this assumption into question.

The first problem arises from the error terms in the regression. To see the nature of this problem let us assume that the

---

[6] As the tax rate falls it becomes increasingly likely that hours of work will rise as there will be a pure substitution effect in the direction of more work. The higher the elasticity of substitution the more likely it is that this will occur, and, if it does occur, the larger the effect will be. See also note 7 below.

[7] If the tax falls far enough this may not be true. If the tax rate fell to the point where the budget constraint was ABI the new equilibrium would be at E_2 where hours would have risen from AH_0 to AH_2.

[8] If the segment changes from BC to BF no *a priori* prediction is possible.

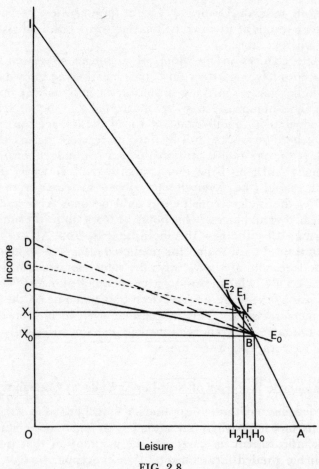

FIG. 2.8

actual budget constraint is ABCD in Fig. 2.9. Suppose we have an individual who works AH_0 hours. If we linearize his budget constraint he will be given the intercept I_1 and the slope w_1. Suppose some other individual with the same budget constraint and the same preferences actually worked AH_{0+u} hours as the result of random error in the model. This individual would be recorded as having the intercept I_2 and the wage rate w_2.

Another problem arises because of measurement error. Suppose AI_1 is calculated as $AI_1 = H_0E - w_1AH_0$. Any errors

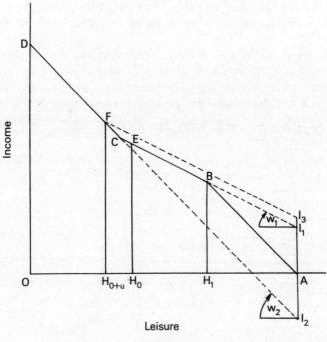

FIG. 2.9

in the measurement of H will cause errors in the measurement of AI_1. Thus if recorded hours exceed actual hours, the recorded intercept will be smaller than the actual intercept. This particular problem of negative correlation between one of the independent variables (AI_1) and the dependent variable H can be avoided[9] if AI_1 is calculated in a way that avoids the use of hours worked. For example, AI_1 could be calculated as $H_1B - w_1AH_1$.

A similar problem arises from error in the measurement of the slope w_1. w_1 is the net marginal wage rate and is probably subject to a fair amount of measurement error.[10] Suppose the individual is at F in Fig. 2.9 and has the net marginal wage w_2. If, to take one example, he reported his net wage

[9] When only one segment of the budget constraint is involved.
[10] The net marginal wage might be estimated directly or it might be computed in various ways. For example gross marginal wage x(1−t) or basic wage rate x overtime premium x(1−t).

rate for the standard working week (w_1) rather than for over-time working his intercept would be calculated as I_3.[11]

I will argue in Chapter 5 that this problem of endogeneity is of sufficient importance that it is useful to group cross-section studies according to the extent to which they recognize this problem and their method of handling it.

[11] Or possibly as I_1 if one used hours at the kink rather than actual hours in the calculation of the intercept.

3
MEASUREMENT PROBLEMS

There are a number of difficulties in applying the theory outlined in Chapters 1 and 2 that can be conveniently dealt with
under the general heading of measurement problems. The
collection is fairly heterogeneous, and is, in total, fairly
daunting.

(a) Sample Selection

There are all the usual problems involved in working from
sample data. At best the results can only be expected to be
relevant to the population studied. This stricture applies to
a large proportion of studies as very few studies have samples
which are representative of the entire population. Many of
the actual studies have been confined to a particular industry,
to managers, to low or to high-income people, to weekly-
paid people, to employees, to retired people, to women, etc.
While it is obvious that the findings related to one population may not be applicable to a different population, it is
perhaps less obvious that the findings may be influenced
by the details of the way the sample is chosen. Suppose for
example that a government wants to know how a new
income maintenance programme for people below some
official poverty line is likely to influence their labour supply.
It might be thought that a study could be carried out more
cheaply by confining the sample to people with incomes below
the poverty line. However such a selection procedure could
miss a major effect of the programme. The reason for this is
that the programme might significantly reduce the labour
supply of people with incomes above the poverty line. The
argument can be illustrated by reference to Fig. 3.1. In the
absence of the income maintenance programme, the individual has the budget constraint AB and is in equilibrium at
E_0 where he has an income OY_0 which is above the poverty
line OP. A negative income tax programme that changed
the budget constraint to DEB would reduce the individual's

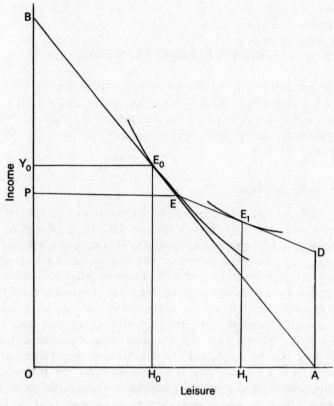

FIG. 3.1

labour supply despite his income being above the poverty line. As the diagram is drawn, the individual reduces his labour supply from AH_0 to AH_1.

There is a further difficulty with sample selection by income limit. Indeed this is a specific instance of a general problem known as truncation bias. If samples are selected by some income rule this also sets a limit of hours worked for each possible wage rate. Now the standard models attempt to explain labour supply in terms of certain financial variables (for example, non-employment income and the wage rate) and a vector of characteristics designed to control for preferences. Typically these variables account for a rather small proportion of the observed variation in

hours of work. A substantial part of the variation in hours is
assumed to depend on an error term in the regression. And if
this error term is randomly distributed there is no particular
problem; however if the error is not randomly distributed the

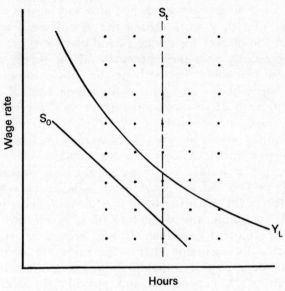

FIG. 3.2

resulting estimates will be biased. The argument is illustrated
in Fig. 3.2. It is assumed that there is a set of observations
for wages and hours shown by the dots in the figure. There is
more than one dot at each wage rate because of the random
error in the model. As the dots are drawn this error is random. The true labour supply fitted to these observations is
S^t which for convenience is assumed to be totally inelastic.
If some upper limit of income is now introduced as a selection criterion only those observations below the line Y_L will
be selected. With these selected observations the observed
supply curve will be a line such as S_0. This line is clearly
biased relative to the true supply curve.

Another problem is whether the sample should be confined to workers or whether it should include all members
of the population even if they are not working. If the sample
is confined to workers it will in general be easier to construct

the budget constraint because the wage rate can be observed. However, if this procedure is followed one will inevitably miss out certain potential variations in labour supply. This is because people can vary their labour supply not only by varying their hours per week but also varying the number of weeks that they work during the year. Even if someone is out of the market for a long period of time this does not mean necessarily that their potential labour supply is zero. It is always possible that such people (housewives, for example) might be induced to join the labour force if offered sufficiently attractive conditions. There will in general be a shadow wage rate for such people which represents the rate at which they would be paid if they were in the labour force. This is potentially of considerable practical importance because, for example, a change in the tax treatment of married women might cause more women to enter the labour force. On the other hand it is obvious that the problems of measuring the wage rate of someone not in the market are quite formidable. This is frequently attempted in practice by assuming that wage rates are determined by basic demographic variables which might include age, education, work experience, and possibly the occupation of one's parents. The difficulties inherent in this approach are discussed in Chapter 7.

(b) The Measure of Work Effort

Work effort is a complex concept which has both a time dimension and an effort per unit of time dimension. The effort dimension is clearly particularly difficult to measure since this requires both a measure of effort itself, and a measure of the wage rate showing the return to that effort. While the theoretical side of incorporation of effort into labour supply has been worked out by Levin, Saunders and Ulph (1975) no adequate measure of effort has yet been made. This means that in practice one must either eliminate from the sample people who are paid by piece rate, bonus or commission in addition to an hourly wage rate, or, if they are left in the sample, recognize that the resulting estimates are likely to be biased. Bias arises because individuals would wish to determine their hours and their effort level simultaneously. The level of effort thus determined will determine their effort payment which will in turn enter into their observed hourly wage rate. It is, of course, still appropriate to ask how an individual would change his hours of work, holding his effort level constant, but it would only be possible to answer this question rigorously if one had some way of holding the effort level constant.

Even if one sets aside the problem of work effort (and this is usually what is done) the problem of measuring the time dimension of work effort is by no means easy. An individual may vary the amount of time that he works in a given year by varying the number of hours that he works per week over a fixed number of weeks, or by varying the number of weeks he works with hours fixed per week, or by some combination of the two. We usually have to rely on individual's reports of the amount of work that they do and this raises considerable problems. The reason, of course, is that memories are short and the accuracy of recollection declines rapidly as the time period lengthens. It would thus be quite unrealistic to ask people to report the number of hours that they had worked each week in the last fifty-two. In practice one is forced to adopt some kind of second-best procedure. One possibility is to ask for hours worked last week which would probably produce a relatively accurate reply. However, 'last' week may be atypical and in any event this leaves out variation in annual hours through variation in weeks worked. Another possibility is to ask for 'normal' or 'usual' hours. The difficulty, of course, with such a question is that it is open to each respondent to put a different interpretation of the meaning of normal; possibilities include: (1) average paid hours (if overtime is paid at twice the normal hourly rate and if the standard working week is 40 hours then the person may be paid for 50 hours when he has actually worked 45); (2) normal hours excluding overtime (40 hours in terms of the previous example); (3) modal hours, or average hours taking into account fluctuations caused by seasonal fluctuations in demand in his industry, his own sickness, or holidays. A third alternative would be to ask individuals only for the number of weeks that they have worked on the assumption that the amount of time worked per week is fixed by the employer. Clearly this procedure depends upon the validity of the last assumption, and if, in fact, employees are free to vary their hours during the week then this last assumption will be invalid.

Thus far we have looked only at the question of hours in the main job. This is entirely consistent with the elementary theory of labour supply which assumes that individuals have to choose between their job and leisure, but there are a variety of reasons why the choice may be more complex, including second jobs or 'moonlighting'. It does seem more consistent with the theory to include all paid jobs in the measure of labour supply but this is not always possible in practice. Another problem is time spent in travelling. Is this to be counted as work or leisure? It is clearly not leisure in the ordinary sense of the word, which might imply that the measure of hours worked should include time from the moment one leaves one's front door until one returns. However, this neglects the possibility that one's employment opportunities may depend upon one's willingness to travel. Perhaps the most serious of all the limitations on the simple work/leisure choice arises because of the existence of non-market work. A man may see himself facing a choice between paid market work, unpaid non-market work (for example, decorating or growing vegetables), and leisure. A woman may see herself facing a choice between market work, housework, and leisure. Clearly the data problems are very different depending upon whether or not one is considering non-market work.

(c) Measures of Non-Employment Income

In the elementary theory of labour supply there is a clear distinction between non-employment income, which is totally independent of the amount of time worked, and employment income, which is directly related to the amount of work done. Variations in non-employment income will have a pure income effect in the elementary theory of labour supply. While the distinction between employment and non-employment income is clear in principle, it is by no means so in practice. In practice it is easy to identify income which does not directly relate to the employment of a single individual; however, it is clear that in many cases such income does not conform to the theoretical construct of non-employment income, and in other cases the conformity is at best dubious. Some of the categories of income not related directly to employment are discussed below. It is difficult to know precisely what to call such income, as it is neither the employment income nor the non-employment income of the simple theory. The term 'other income' is a convenient shorthand for this third category of income.

One of the important forms of other income is state benefits which are income-related or means-tested. Such benefits can take a wide variety of forms, such as a payment in cash (Family Income Supplement in the UK), or in kind (free school meals) made to families whose income falls below some specified level. Another example is reduced outlays for people with low incomes (for example, rent and rate rebates in the UK). All these schemes make it possible for the recipients to have a higher level of consumption than they could have in the absence of the programmes, and entitlement depends upon some measure of income. This means that if the recipient works more he will have some extra employment income but he will lose some of his other income. While it is wrong to neglect such income, it is also wrong to treat it as if it were true non-employment income. From one point of view the proper way of treating other income is to model its effects on the budget constraint very carefully. However this neglects the problem of misconceptions, which is discussed below.

A second category of other income is the employment income of other household members. The nature of the problem depends upon whether one is using a household model or an individual model. The problem in the context of the household model is discussed in Chapter 8 and here attention is confined to an individual model. The problem with income from other members of the household in the context of an individual model is that it violates the basic assumption of the model that the individual is an independent agent. If household labour supply decisions are made simultaneously by all members of the household 'other income' may depend in part on hours worked by the individual. In these circumstances such income will not have a pure income effect.

A final class of other income is the income from capital. Included in this category would be interest and dividend income, rental income, imputed income from house ownership, etc. At first sight it may appear that income in this category is much closer to the theoretical construct of non-employment income, but it is at least possible that this is not so. Income from capital depends upon the ownership of capital and while this may be taken as approximately constant in the very short run, it would be inappropriate to do so in a life-cycle context. If we are including interest receipts we should include interest payments as well. The amount of money that someone *wishes* to borrow may well depend on his expected income which in turn would depend on how long he intends to work. In addition one's *ability* to borrow may also depend upon one's income, or on the lender's perception of one's future income, which in turn may be dependent on past income and past hours. Therefore it may well be the case that there is no empirical counterpart to the theoretical construct of non-employment income.

There are other more practical problems with the measurement of income from capital. How does one define capital and the income arising from it? Capital gains and losses ought to be included. If there is no money illusion such gains clearly ought to be included on a real basis, but should they be included on a real basis if there is money illusion? Should gains be included on an accrued or a realized basis? Imputed income from home ownership ought to be included, but there are measurement problems similar to those outlined above. In addition allowance is needed for the cost of repairs, etc. After one has sorted out the conceptual problems with other income there remain daunting problems involved with the collection of the information. Collecting the data necessary to model means-tested benefits, the income from other household members, and income from capital would require a great deal of detailed information. People may be unwilling to disclose this information, and evidence from the Stirling survey suggests that people may be unwilling to disclose information about other household members, particularly when the respondent is not the head of the household. Even if people are willing to disclose the information it may be difficult to frame questions that they can understand, or they may not know the information that is wanted. Even if they are willing to provide small amounts of detailed information they may get fed up with too many questions, which means that there may be a trade-off between obtaining the amount of detailed information that is wanted and keeping the questionnaire sufficiently simple to achieve a reasonably high response rate.

(d) The Wage Rate

It should be clear from the theoretical discussions in Chapters 1 and 2 that the wage rate that is required is the net marginal wage rate. For the individual this is the wage rate after taking into account, where relevant, the basic wage rate, the overtime premium, income taxation, social security taxes, means-tested social benefits, and the wage rate on second jobs. The data requirements are again large and as suggested in the previous section there may be a trade-off between completeness of data and response rate. However, it is clear that measuring the wage rate by dividing gross income by hours worked is unsatisfactory. The reasons for this are given in Chapter 2 and in Chapter 5.

(e) Existing Data Sets

The problems that have been discussed earlier have to be faced in a particularly acute form when choosing between using an existing data set or not doing the work at all. This choice may be forced upon one by considerations of money or time or inclination or some combination of the three. Probably no set of data is ideal for this purpose (including ones specially collected for labour supply analysis) but there are degrees of departure from the ideal. Not surprisingly, when the first studies of labour supply were made, the measurement problems which have been discussed in this chapter were not fully appreciated, and it seems fairly clear, in retrospect, that some of the early studies were done on sets of data which were so inadequate that no reliable estimates of labour supply could be obtained from them. Nevertheless it may have been quite useful for the attempt to have been made because of what has been learned about data requirements.

(f) General Problems

I would like to end this chapter with a discussion of three general problems.

The identification problem

The identification problem can be simply stated. If people are observed to be working certain hours at various wage rates, are we observing positions on a supply curve, a demand curve, or a mixture of both? Clearly one is most likely to observe points off the supply curve if workers are unable to work their equilibrium hours. This is one reason why constraints are important.

Misconceptions

The discussion so far has proceeded on the assumption that individuals fully understand their budget constraints. It should be clear from the discussion in this and the previous chapter that budget constraints are extremely complex and affected by the tax-transfer system in a variety of ways. It is clear from survey work that individuals do not in fact understand their budget constraints at all accurately (see, for example, Brown (1968) and Brown and Jackson (1978), pages 265–67). Very little work has been done on the extent to which behaviour is influenced by misconceptions about budget constraints. A notable exception is a paper by Harvey Rosen (1976). Rosen estimates a variable for tax illusion and concludes that the extent of illusion is small. Work at Stirling University has also failed to find any evidence of behaviour being altered by misconceptions, but it does seem to be an area of sufficient importance for further work to be done.

Questionnaire data

There remains a fundamental question about all data collected by questionnaires and much data collected by other methods. The question is this, 'Do people really answer the questions that are asked?' There are a whole variety of reasons why individuals may not. They may understand the question and give a deliberately misleading answer because, for example, they may think the person asking the question is a representative of the taxation department and that the correct answer may lead to a higher tax liability; or they may give a misleading answer because they think it is more acceptable socially. People may also give misinformation because their memories are fallible or because it takes too much trouble to turn to files which have accurate information. As Sir Josiah Stamp once said: 'The Government are very keen on amassing statistics. They collect them, add them, raise them to the nth power, take the cubed root and prepare wonderful diagrams. But you must never forget that everyone of these figures comes in the first instance from the village watchman, who just puts down what he damned pleases'. Even when the individual is asked questions about himself he may put down 'what he damned pleases'.

The problem is in a sense worse, although the result the same, if the individual does not understand the question which has been asked, or if he interprets it differently from the way that the researcher intended. It is well known that subtle differences in question wording can affect the responses fairly significantly. It is sometimes very clear that questions have been misunderstood. For example, in the pilot work for the Stirling survey it became clear that many of the potential respondents did not understand such technical terms as *gross, net, percentage, proportion, average*, etc. Even when the questions are asked in a very non-technical way the problem can arise. For example, in the Stirling survey respondents were shown a card which showed income in bands, and were then asked, 'Could you show me the group on this card that gives the total amount of money normally coming into the house each week, counting all wages and salaries after deductions and other things like Family Allowances, Pensions and so on?' What was wanted from this question was the total net household income. Some respondents gave an answer which was 10% or less of their own take-home pay. It seems likely that they had interpreted the question to mean total net take-home pay excluding their own take-home pay. In this particular case the misunderstanding on the part of some respondents was easy to identify because of other information collected. In other cases there may be no information available as a cross-check.

(g) Conclusion

Clearly measurement problems are formidable. It is important that the practitioners and the users of research work in this area should understand the difficulties. Practitioners have an obligation both to minimize measurement problems so far as that is possible, and to make the users aware of the extent to which the problems cannot be resolved.

4

THE INTERVIEW APPROACH

This chapter plus the next two will review the empirical evidence on the effects of taxation on the labour supply of men. Each of the chapters is devoted to one of the three main methodologies that have been employed. The present chapter is devoted to the interview approach, where the analysis starts from questions in which respondents are asked how their behaviour has been affected by taxation. Various tests are then applied in an attempt to eliminate implausible answers. It has been widely recognized that this approach could lead to an overestimate of tax effects if, for example, people thought it was socially acceptable to blame the tax system for not working harder. But the bias could work the other way. It is possible that people's behaviour is affected by tax but that they are unaware of it. For example, people may have the correct 'feel' for the shape and position of their budget constraints without being aware of the role of taxes in their unconscious process. Here I consider first two large-scale studies of British low-income groups and then look at British and American evidence about high-come groups.

(1) Interview Studies–Low-Income Groups

There have been two large-scale British surveys of low-income groups using the interview approach. In the early 1950s the British Royal Commission on the Taxation of Profits and Income (1954) commissioned a survey by the Government Social Survey. The sample included industrial workers and supervisors in England and Wales who were able to vary their labour supply either because they could work overtime or because they were paid piece rates. In all, 1,203 men and 226 women were interviewed and these were thought to be representative of about half of the total labour force. It was argued in the report that: 'Behaviour may be related (a) to

accurate knowledge of the factors or (b) to incorrect information which is believed to be true or (c) it may reflect
attitudes which are believed to be true or (d) it may reflect
attitudes which are not directly associated with any specific
facts at all'. Under (a) the report concluded that there was
no evidence that productive effort was inhibited by the
income tax. This conclusion came from studying a subsample of workers who claimed to know all of the following:
whether or not they paid tax, the tax rate that they paid
(including zero), and about how much more they could earn
before paying tax at a higher rate. This sub-sample was then
asked, 'Would it be worth your while to earn more if it meant
going on to a higher rate of tax?' Unfortunately, this key
question could not produce meaningful answers. If people
are free to choose how long they wish to work they will
move to a position of equilibrium with the budget constraint
determined by their present tax rate. Clearly someone in
equilibrium will not find it worth while to move. The report
found under (b) and (c) that opinions about tax had a slight
but statistically significant association with work but that
knowledge of facts (whether or not tax is paid) was not significantly associated with variation in hours.

Some twenty years later Brown and Levin collected and
analysed data from over 2,000 weekly-paid workers in
Britain. After a large number of factual and attitudinal questions about work, in which tax was *not* mentioned by the
interviewer, respondents were asked if tax had made them
work 'more overtime', 'less overtime', or 'doesn't apply/
neither'. The replies for men are shown in section 1 of Table
4.1 where it can be seen that 74 per cent claimed no effect,
15 per cent claimed tax had made them work more and 11
per cent claimed tax had made them work less.

Brown and Levin then decided whether or not these claims
were plausible using the general rule that an employee's
claim was plausible unless demonstrably inconsistent with
earlier statements. For example, people who claimed 'less
overtime' were judged implausible if they would not work
more overtime at a higher overtime rate than they were
currently being paid. Those judged to be plausible are shown
in section II of the table where it can be seen that a larger

proportion of men claiming 'more' were judged to be plausible (173 out of 205) than of men claiming 'less' (88 out of 199). In practice, employees may not be free to choose the amount of overtime that they would like to work. Perhaps the clearest and most common form of constraint is that an employee may be required by his employer to work longer or shorter hours than he himself wishes to. Thirty per cent of men were constrained by this definition. In addition to this situation, which was called a 'work' constraint, there are two other classes that may be considered constrained as well. One of these is termed the 'pay' constraint. If a person's total pay does not change because of the number of hours he works, then the tax system cannot really be making him work more or less overtime. With one exception, Brown and Levin treated all workers not paid extra for overtime as being constrained (the exception is where people who are not paid extra for overtime said they chose the job because it did not have any overtime): 9 per cent of men had a pay constraint. The final type of constraint used is a constraint termed 'personal'. An employee may wish to work overtime but for reasons of health or family commitments (for example, a married woman with a young child) may not be able to. Six per cent of men had a personal constraint.

The results are given in section III of Table 4.1 The most dramatic change from excluding the constrained occurs in the number of overtime hours worked by married men with children claiming to be unaffected by tax. Brown and Levin concluded:

the number of hours worked 'last week' by those claiming tax had made them work more overtime is consistently greater than the number of overtime hours worked by those claiming that tax had made them work less overtime, and in all cases those claiming 'more' work more overtime than those claiming 'neither'. In most cases those claiming 'less' work less overtime than those claiming 'neither'.

The evidence clearly suggests, therefore, that the aggregate effect of tax on overtime is small; it may perhaps add about 1% to the total hours worked, since on balance tax has made people work more rather than less overtime. (pp. 846-7)

(2) Interview Studies–High-Income Earners

There have been two studies in Britain of high-income indi-

Table 4.1 Claimed effects on tax on overtime hours and actual mean overtime hours worked

Demog. group	Claim	I All claims			II High plausible			III High plausible and unconstrained		
		N	%c	Mean over-time hours	N	%c	Mean over-time hours	N	%c	Mean over-time hours
All men	Less	149	11	3·5	88	7	3·4	61	9	2·8b
	Neither	987	74	4·2	987	79	4·2	470	69	6·2
	More	205	15	9·0b	173	14	10·6b	151	22	10·6b
Single men	Less	44	13	2·5	25	8	2·8	19	12	2·3
	Neither	259	77	2·2	259	84	2·2	123	75	3·5
	More	32	10	3·1	24	8	3·3a	23	14	4·0
Married men without children	Less	54	12	3·8	33	8	4·1	22	10	3·1
	Neither	339	73	4·3	339	78	4·3	153	68	5·9
	More	69	15	9·9b	60	14	11·3b	51	23	11·2b
Married men with children	Less	45	9	3·8	26	6	2·3a	17	6	1·8b
	Neither	353	72	5·6	353	77	5·6	182	68	8·6
	More	94	19	9·5b	80	17	11·2b	69	26	11·1a

Notes: aSignificant at 5 per cent.
bSignificant at 1 per cent.
cPercentages are of the demographic group in the relevant column. Thus in the high plausible column the 173 men claiming 'more' are 14 per cent of all high plausible men, but only 13 per cent of all men.

Source: Brown and Levin (1974).

viduals which are particularly interesting because both studied the same professions. A survey of British solicitors and accountants conducted by George F. Break in 1956 found a small but significant number of persons experiencing net tax effects; but he did not find the disincentive effect (13.1 per cent of the sample) to be significantly greater than the incentive effect (10.1 per cent of sample). He concluded that the net effect 'be it disincentive or incentive, is not large enough to be of great economic or sociological significance'.

In 1969 D. B. Fields and W. T. Stanbury repeated Break's study. They found 18·9 per cent of the sample experienced disincentive effects and 11·2 per cent experienced incentive effects. Unlike Break's findings, the difference in these proportions was statistically significant. Furthermore, the difference in the proportions experiencing a disincentive effect over the twelve-year period between the two surveys (from 13·1 to 18·9 per cent) was statistically significant. Thus Fields and Stanbury's results suggest that, if there is a net tax effect, it is likely to be in the direction of a disincentive, and also that the disincentive effect is growing stronger over time.

This would have been a reasonable conclusion were it not for problems of comparability between these two studies. Fields and Stanbury claim to have repeated Break's study but there were important differences.

(1) In Break's study the interviewer, without mentioning taxation, asked the respondent his reasons for doing the amount of work he was doing, then asked questions about tax influences on his work, and then questioned the respondent about his marginal rate of tax and his income. Fields and Stanbury reversed the order of these questions and asked the respondents about their marginal tax rate and income *before* asking questions about tax influences on work, thereby sensitizing their respondents to tax effects in a way that Break had not done.

(2) Fields and Stanbury inserted questions about Capital Gains Tax, the Special Charge and Selective Employment Tax just before asking the respondents about the effect of tax on their work, whereas Break's interviewers had not even mentioned the word 'taxation' in any of their questions be-

Table 4.2 Effect of hypothetical tax on particular areas of executive effort

	Effort on primary job		Vacation		Family members in labour force		'Little ventures' and consulting		Retirement	
	No.	%	No.	%	No.	%	No.	%	No.	%
Top executives—large companies										
(a) None	17	94	17	94	16	88	13	72	11	61
(b) Harder	0	0	1	6	1	6	4	22	2	11
(c) Less hard	0	0	0	0	1	6	1	6	5	28
(d) No answer	1	6	0	0	0	0	0	0	0	0
Top executives—small companies										
(a) None	8	53	11	73	12	80	12	80	8	53
(b) Harder	4	27	2	14	0	0	2	13	0	0
(c) Less hard	1	7	1	7	1	7	0	0	4	27
(d) No answer	2	13	1	7	2	13	1	7	3	20
Middle management										
(a) None	21	81	24	92	24	92	17	65	15	58
(b) Harder	5	19	2	8	1	4	8	31	2	8
(c) Less hard	0	0	0	0	0	0	1	4	9	34
(d) No answer	0	0	0	0	1	4	0	0	0	0

Cross-section										
(a) None	14	93	14	93	13	87	10	67	13	87
(b) Harder	2	14	1	7	2	13	5	33	2	13
(c) Less hard	0	0	0	0	0	0	0	0	0	0
(d) No answer	0	0	0	0	0	0	0	0	0	0
Total sample										
(a) None	59	80	66	89	65	88	52	70	47	64
(b) Harder	11	15	6	8	4	5	19	26	6	8
(c) Less hard	1	1	1	1	2	3	2	3	18	24
(d) No answer	3	4	1	1	3	4	1	1	3	4

(Data in cells are percentages of each category of executive affected as indicated in each area of effort.)

Notes

Top executives—large companies are the chief executive officers of companies numbered among the very largest on Fortune's list of Industrials (manufacturing), finance, retailing or public utility companies.

Top executives—small companies are the senior executive officers in smaller companies (generally manufacturing firms), developers and 'seasoned observers of the business scene' (investment bankers, men on corporate boards, or consultants).

Middle management are middle managers, both upper (senior) and lower (junior) generally between 32 and 50 years old, characteristically with larger companies, and considered promising executive material by their employers.

Cross-section is a widely-ranging cross-section of executives in two cities with a recent record of rapid growth.

Source: Holland (1977).

fore asking about the influence of tax on their work.

(3) Fields and Stanbury asked questions 'relating to the incentive or disincentive effects on work effort of high marginal rates of income tax', whereas Break had asked questions about 'tax influences' on work effort. A subtle point, but one wonders how the results would have been affected if Fields and Stanbury had substituted the word 'average' for 'marginal' or better still just left it out altogether. The words used imply bias because high *marginal* tax rates are relevant to disincentive effects while the *average* rate of tax is relevant to the incentive effect.

Any one of these three criticisms would cast doubt on the validity of a comparison between the two studies; and the three criticisms together make me unwilling to accept Fields and Stanbury's conclusions from the evidence they have presented. This, of course, does not rule out the possibility that their conclusions are broadly correct despite criticisms of their approach.

Barlow, Brazer and Morgan (1966) studied 957 'affluent' Americans who had incomes of over $10,000 in 1961. Their sampling procedure was stratified to give a higher proportion of interviews in the highest income groups. Their respondents were asked if income taxes had affected 'how much work you (or your wife) do' and, if any effect were claimed, to give an example. Twelve per cent of the total sample claimed that taxes made them work less. The proportion claiming disincentives varied from 2 per cent to 84 per cent among various sub-groups. The group with the highest disincentives were people under 65 without dependent children who were conscious of taxes and who had opportunities to work more. Barlow, Brazer and Morgan regarded about half of the reported disincentives as 'illusory or negligible'. They concluded:

The survey revealed that those reporting a plausible disincentive received 6 per cent of the aggregate income of the high-income group, or about 2·5 per cent of total income in the economy. The survey also revealed that those reporting a plausible disincentive worked on the average about five-sixths as many hours during the year as did the rest of the high-income persons in the labor force. Thus on the basis of the assumptions cited above, it follows that the total loss of annual output in the economy in 1963 due to the existence of the progressive income tax instead of some feasible alternative may have been of the order of one-third of 1 per cent. (pp. 145-6)

Holland interviewed 125 US executives. His study is particularly interesting for unlike other interview studies he attempted to measure the substitution effect directly. He asked his respondents to consider how they would react to a hypothetical tax in which tax liability would depend for each individual on his 'inherent capacity to generate income [as measured by a battery of tests], not his zeal in doing so ....' (Holland, 1977, p. 44). His findings are summarized in Table 4.2 where it can be seen that 15 per cent of the sample claimed that they would work harder with a zero marginal rate tax.

Conclusions

Table 4.3 summarizes results from a number of interview

Table 4.3 *Interview studies-summary of results*

	Proportion Claiming net Disincentive	Proportion Claiming net Incentive
Low Income		
Brown and Levin (1974)	11	15
High Income		
Break (1957)	13	10
Fields and Stanbury (1971)	19	11
Barlow, Brazer, and Morgan (1966)	12	not reported
Holland (1977)	15	1*a

*aThis figure is *not* comparable with the other figures in the column (see text for explanation of Holland's hypothetical tax).

studies. Between about one-tenth and one-fifth of those interviewed were found to have a disincentive effect. It is not surprising to find the lowest proportion in the Brown and Levin study, as the workers they interviewed had relatively low marginal tax rates, and as these workers have relatively low incomes the high proportion of incentive cases is not unexpected. Given the questions asked by Fields and Stanbury and by Holland it is hardly surprising that they found the highest proportion of those claiming disincentives.[1]

As these results contain no elasticities their quantitative importance is difficult to judge. The authors of the studies typically have concluded that the results are small. There are three reasons why this may not be the appropriate conclusion. Firstly, despite our criticisms of their methods, Fields and Stanbury may have been right in finding a move over time towards a disincentive effect. Secondly, this move might well have gathered pace as inflation has changed the real tax system. Finally, the samples of high-income people may all be biased against the finding of disincentives. If there were disincentives from tax some people would be expected to leave countries with high rates and others would be expected to choose less demanding occupations with lower incomes. Neither of these groups would appear in the specially selected high-income samples.

The interview technique has a number of disadvantages. When an emotive subject like taxation is being studied there are a number of potential pitfalls. Respondents may try to mislead the interviewers; their replies may reflect popular prejudices or misconceptions about taxation rather than their own genuine beliefs. While these dangers can be minimized by careful construction of the interview schedule, there remains the possibility that people may not understand how tax affects them. Minimizing one set of problems may create another. Brown and Levin (like many others) started their interview schedule with factual questions to provide a check on the later questions about the effects of tax. This meant that they restricted to one interview a household because subsequent interviewees might have learnt that the interviews were about taxation. Multiple interviews would have provided better factual data for household labour supply models.

Most interview studies have reported the proportion of the sample having net incentive and disincentive effects. This has

---

[1] On the basis of questions asked Holland should have found the highest proportion of disincentives.

the advantage of making it clear that tax effects may differ for different people, but it has the disadvantage of not providing separate estimates of income and substitution effects. This may however be more a criticism of particular studies than of the method, for Holland estimated substitution effects separately. It does however seem unlikely that one can expect to find accurate estimates of elasticities using this method. A further difficulty is that the relatively small proportion reporting tax effects means that a very large sample may be required to produce enough data for sophisticated analysis.

5

CROSS–SECTION ECONOMETRIC STUDIES ON MEN

Over the last decade the most widely used method of estimating labour supply has been cross-section econometric studies. In this approach some measure of labour supply (say hours) is regressed on certain variables to represent the budget constraint (say the wage rate and non-employment income) and other variables (say age and education) are added to control for preferences. If the control variables hold preferences constant, then variation in hours will depend on differences between individuals in their budget constraints. Thus if the only difference between individuals was in their wage rate, differences in labour supply would be attributed to this difference. It is then inferred that it is possible to predict how individuals will behave over time from the differences between individuals at a single point in time. Suppose there are two people: A with a wage of w who worked H hours and B with a wage of 2w who worked 1·5H hours. The inference would be that if a 50 per cent tax was put on B that he would reduce his hours to H.

Three Types of Econometric Study

When Godfrey surveyed work on labour supply (Godfrey 1975) he found little variance in the way in which the models were specified. He wrote: 'As well as the general agreement about the appropriate theoretical basis, researchers have also differed very little in their specification of labour supply functions. The model established by Kosters (1966) has been the standard framework for almost all of the published work . . .' (p. 54). While this remains true of the majority of econometric work it is now clear that the Kosters' model is seriously defective.

There have been two types of attempt, of increasing complexity, to deal with the deficiencies of Kosters' model. It is convenient to refer to the studies that employ the Kosters model as Type I studies and to refer to the later studies as

Type II and Type III.

Type I studies

There have been a large number of Type I studies and they have varied in a number respects such as data source, measure of labour supply, preference variables included, the definitions and measurement of non-employment income, functional form estimated etc. Despite this variation they all employ the same theoretical framework and a similar specification.

I will argue that the distinguishing feature of the Type I studies is this common framework and that this framework is fundamentally defective. That being the case the detailed differences in approach are not of great interest and are not included and the studies are represented by a single example discussed in some detail with a sample of other results presented to give some indication of the range of estimates obtained.

The essence of the Type I approach is that it employs the very simple theoretical structure outlined in Chapter 1. Labour supply (H) is assumed to depend on the wage rate (w) (w), non-employment income (NEY), taste variables (X_1 to X_n) and a random error term u. Thus

$$H = H(w, NEY, X_1 \ldots X_n, u).$$

This is frequently estimated in a linear form, for example

$$H = a_1 w + a_2 NEY + a_3 X_1 \ldots + a_n X_n + u$$

A recent Type I study is the book by Stanley Masters and Irwin Garfinkel (1977). This study is taken to represent the Type I studies because it is recent and in general very carefully done. Masters and Garfinkel employ a large number of alternative measures of labour supply, two measures of non-employment income, and two measures of the wage rate. They do their estimates on two different data sets and on a variety of demographic groups. Space precludes reporting all their results and those reported here refer to one data set (that from the Survey of Economic Opportunity), one measure of labour supply (hours worked in the survey week), and one definition of the wage rate (the log normal wage rate) of prime-age males.

The relevant regression was as follows:

$$HwK_{sw} = a_1 + a_2NEY + a_3OTHERN + a_4LNWR + a_5HPRELY$$
$$+ a_6HLIMLY + a_7HPRE + a_8HLIMA + a_9HLIMK$$
$$+ a_{10}HLIMKA + a_{11} BLACK + a_{12}OTHRACE + a_{13}FAMSIZ$$
$$+ a_{14}PENDUM + a_{15}NTWTH.$$

The variables are defined as follows:

NEY = Nonemployment income. Reported NEY in the SEO includes family income from (a) Social Security (Old Age, Survivors', and Disability Insurance (OASDI)) or Railroad retirement, (b) pensions from civil service, military, and private retirement programs, (c) veterans' pension or compensation (VP), (d) public assistance, relief, or welfare from state or local governments (PA), (e) Unemployment Insurance (UI), (f) Workers' Compensation, illness, or accident benefits (WC), (g) interest, (h) dividends, (i) rent, and (j) other regular income such as payments from annuities, royalties, private welfare, or relief, contributions from persons not living in the household, and alimony or armed forces allotments.

LNWR = Natural logarithm of the reported hourly wage rate. For the SEO it is defined as normal weekly earnings divided by actual hours worked during the survey week.

OTHERN = annual earnings of other family members.

NTWTH = The net worth of a family's total assets that bear no monetary return.

HPRELY = A dummy variable with a value of one if health prevented the individual from working at all the previous year.

HLIMLY = A dummy variable wih a value of 1 if health prevented the individual from working part (but not all) of the previous year.

HPRE = A dummy variable with a value of 1 if the individual has a long-term health disability that prevents him from working.

HLIMA = A dummy variable with a value of 1 if the individual has a long-term health disability that limits the amount of work he can do.

HLIMK = A dummy variable with a value of 1 if the individual has a long-term health disability that limits the kind

Table 5.1 *Various point estimates of income and substitution parameters for males*

Author	Data source-year	Race–marital status–age group	Substitution elasticity	Total-income elasticity
Ashenfelter and Heckman	SEO*1967	Husbands 25 to 64, wives not working	·12	-·27
	SMSA aggregates in Census—1960	Male labour-force participation rates for SMSAs	·06	-·06
Boskin	SEO—1967	Husbands 20 to 59	·10 (white) <0 (black)	-·17 (white) -·06 (black) estimated
Cohen, Rea Lerman	CPS†—1967	Males 22 to 54	Negative	-·08 to + ·03
Fleisher, Parsons, and Porter	National Longitudinal Survey, 1966–67	Urban husbands 45 to 59, "full" sample excluding men who received work-conditioned nonemployment income	·04 -·19	-·23 -·08
Garfinkel**	SEO—1967	Able-bodied husbands 25 to 61 in labour force	Near 0 (sometimes positive and sometimes negative)	Near 0 (sometimes positive and sometimes negative)
Greenberg and Kosters	SEO—1967	Married males in labour force <$62; income <$15,000	·02 to + ·20 (authors' preference: ·20)	-·15 to -·34 (authors' preference: -·29)

Hall	SEO*–1967	Husbands 20 to 59 with predicted wage per hour < $3.00	−·20 to +·39 Weighted ave. = ·06 (white) −·68 to +·25 Weighted ave. = −·10 (black)	−·24 to −·51 (white) −·12 to −·28 (black)
Hill	SEO–1967	Males 25 to 54, income below poverty line — income above poverty line	·47 (white) ·27 (black) ·52 (white) ·56 (black)	−·68 (white) −·35 (black) −·86 (white) −·88 (black)
Kalachek and Raines	CPS†–1966	Males 24 to 61 income < $8,500	·86 (white) ·96 (nonwhite)	−·31 to −·33
Parker	SEO–1967	Males with children, below poverty line — above poverty line	0 (full year, full time) ·34 (full year, part time) −·05 (full year, full time) ·27 (full year, part time)	−·04 −·34 ·001 to −·15
Rosen and Welch	·001 Sample in Census—1960	Employed husbands 25 to 65, income < $10,000	(range: negative to ·6) ave. = −·2 to ·3	·001 to −·15
Tella, Tella, and Green	SEO–1967	Male heads, 18 to 64, wage per hour < $3.00	·16 to ·45 (authors' preference: ·16 to ·18)	−·11 to −·38 (authors' preference −·11 to −·16)

* Survey of Economic Opportunity
† Consumer Price Survey
Source: Cain and Watts (1978)

of work he can do.

HLIMKA   = A dummy variable with a value of 1 if the individual
                has a long-term health disability that limits the kind
                and amount of work he can do.

BLACK   = A dummy variable with a value of 1 if the individual
                is black.

OTHRACE   = A dummy variable with a value of 1 if the individual
                is neither black nor white.

FAMSIZ   = A linear variable for family size.

PENDUM   = A dummy variable with value of 1 if the individual
                has a pension (SR) or if the individual lived in an
                interview unit in which there was income from
                pensions but in which no one else was retired (SEO).
                (pp. 30, 276-7)

The authors do not report the R^2 or significance of the
equation as a whole or the coefficients of most of the variables but they do report the following coefficients (with t
statistics): NEY ·00043(2·2); OTHERN ·00002(2·3); LNWR
6·6(14·1). The price elasticity is given as −0·16, the income
elasticity as 0·10, and the substitution elasticity as −0·8. It
may be noted that the income elasticity should be negative if
income and leisure are normal goods and that the substitution elasticity should always be positive. (Other results not
reported have different signs and in some cases these other
signs conform to the predictions of theory.) Table 5.1 from
Cain and Watts (1973) reports results from various other
cross-section studies most of which are Type I studies (the
study by Hall is a Type II study—see below). Because of the
weaknesses inherent in the Type I studies which are explained below the detailed differences between these studies
are not explored.

Masters and Garfinkel note a number of ways in which
the definitions of their variables may be defective. The definition of NEY includes income-related benefits such as
public assistance. As we saw in Chapter 3 such income-
related benefits do not conform to the theoretical construct
of non-employment income and Masters and Garfinkel have
eliminated from the sample people with such income-related
non-employment income.

The earnings of other family members (OTHERN) is included as a separate variable in the equations. Masters and

Garfinkel recognize that household labour supply decisions may be taken jointly and thus that these earnings do not conform to the theoretical construct (see Chapter 3).

The wage rate employed is a gross average wage rate found by dividing gross income by hours. As the fundamental defect of the Type I studies derives from the use of this variable it is worth quoting extensively from Masters and Garfinkel's discussion. In the quotation that follows they explain how the wage rate is defined and the problems that arise from measurement errors:

The hourly wage rate in the SEO is constructed by dividing normal weekly earnings by actual hours worked during the survey week. This wage rate variable presents two major problems. First, it is missing for all individuals who did not work for wages during the survey week. Thus for demographic groups in which most members do not work, such as men 72 or older, no measure of the hourly wage exists for large portions of the sample. Even for groups like prime-age married men in which almost everyone works, however, dividing normal earnings by actual hours worked may create serious measurement errors in the wage rate variable. The hourly wage rate is too low for all individuals who worked more hours in the survey week than their normal work week and too high for all individuals who worked fewer hours than their normal work week. This kind of measurement error will normally bias the wage rate coefficient toward zero.* When hours worked during the survey week is the dependent variable, however, the wage rate will be negatively correlated with the error term and a negative bias will result.

* There are some other, less important, sources of measurement error. Perhaps the most important of these stems from the confusion between gross and net earnings. Although interviewers were instructed to obtain normal gross weekly earnings, there is undoubtedly some error due to confusion between gross and net, since many individuals know only their take-home pay. Experience in the New Jersey Income-Maintenance Experiment suggests that it takes many interviews for families to learn the distinction well and to report gross earnings consistently.

Masters and Garfinkel thus believe that their estimate of price elasticity is too large a negative number.

It will be noted in the footnote quoted above that the researchers went to a great deal of trouble to insure that their income measure was *gross*: Masters and Garfinkel state that it would have been better to use net income:

Next let us consider the effects of using gross income rather than an income measure that is net of taxes and working expenses. Let us start with the relatively simple case of a proportional income tax. In this case, a given percentage change in the gross wage will be equivalent to the same percentage change in the net wage. Therefore, when a logarithmic form of the wage variable is used [as in Eq. (3.1)], a relatively small proportional tax will not bias our results. To the extent that our tax structure is progressive, however, our wage rate coefficients will be smaller in absolute value than they should be. Moreover, our estimates of the income effect will be a little too small in absolute value even if the tax is proportional, since these estimates are based on linear coefficients.†

† 'If there is a proportional tax rate of t, our income effect estimates should be increased by a factor of 1+t. Although we would have preferred to use data on each source of income after taxes, such information was not reported in our data sets. Making detailed tax rate adjustments is beyond the scope of this study. Rather than making a simple, inaccurate adjustment we prefer to make no adjustment at all.' (p. 45).

While the Masters and Garfinkel study is careful, with the authors taking considerable care to point to possible biases in their results, they fail to recognize two interrelated fundamental difficulties with their analysis. Other Type I studies have the same problems.

The first problem is that the theoretical model they use is improperly specified when budget constraints are non-linear. The argument is illustrated with reference to Fig. 5.1. Suppose there are two individuals who have the same non-employment income (AB), the same tax threshold (OX), and who face the same tax rate (t) for incomes above the threshold. Individual 1 has a job where he is paid extra for hours in excess of the standard working week (AS). In the absence of tax his budget constraint is ABCD. With tax his budget constraint is ABFGH and he is in equilibrium at E_1. Individual 2 is not paid extra for overtime. In the absence of tax, his budget constraint is ABI; with tax the budget constraint is ABJK and he is in equilibrium at E_2. The Type I models would assign to both of these individuals the same non-employment income (AB: which is correct) and the same gross average wage (which leads to difficulties). It will be remembered that the wage rate is defined as gross income divided by hours. For individual 1 this is

$$w = \frac{LM}{AH_1} = \frac{LM}{BL}$$

and for the second individual

$$w = \frac{PN}{AH_2} = \frac{PN}{BN}.$$

Thus

$$w = \frac{LM}{AH_1} = \frac{PN}{AH_2}.$$

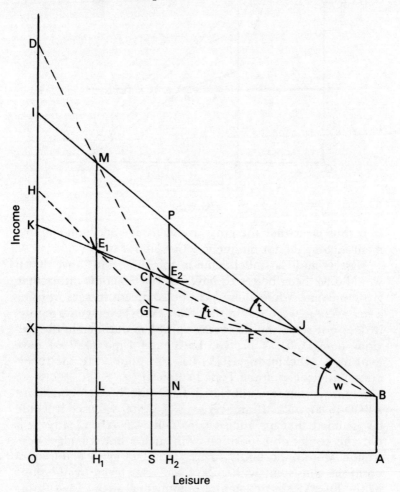

FIG. 5.1

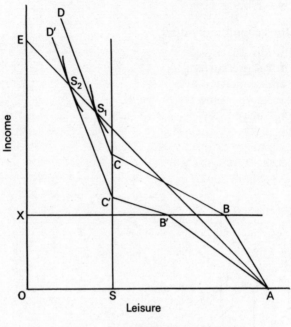

FIG. 5.2

It is thus clear that the gross average wage and non-employment income do not uniquely define labour supply.

Masters and Garfinkel argue in the quotation above that it would have been better to have used net income rather than gross income. While there may be some advantages in using a net average wage rate rather than a gross average wage rate, it does not solve the theoretical problem outlined in the previous paragraph, as Brown, Levin and Ulph (1974a) have explained. (Dickinson (1975) has also pointed to the theoretical deficiencies in the Type I studies.)

Suppose that an individual faces the budget constraint ABCD in Fig. 5.2. If an average wage rate was used it would be assumed that his budget constraint was AE. Clearly S_1 is not the equilibrium position with such a linear budget constraint. More importantly, there are in fact many equilibrium positions consistent with an average wage given by the slope of the line AE. For example, an individual with a lower gross wage rate but the same tax threshold and overtime premium could have a budget constraint such as AB′C′D′ and be in equilibrium S_2. Thus the average wage rate and non-employment income do not uniquely determine hours worked.

In addition to the theoretical problem just outlined the Type I procedure suffers from endogeneity bias (see Chapter 3). This endogeneity bias exists in addition to the bias caused by measurement error mentioned by Masters and Garfinkel. If budget constraints are non-linear both the gross and the net average wage depend upon hours worked (rather than hours depending on the wage). The problem is illustrated for two different types of non-linear budget constraints in Fig. 5.3 and 5.4 which for simplicity are drawn on the assumption

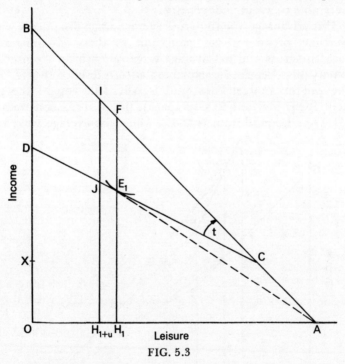

FIG. 5.3

that non-employment income is zero. In Fig. 5.3 the only non-linearity is caused by the tax (t) on incomes above the exemption level. If equilibrium is at E_1, Type I models using a gross wage would use the slope of AB as the wage and those using a net wage would use the slope of AE_1 as the wage.

Suppose that from the random error in the model someone works H_{1+u} hours. In this case the net wage would be given by the slope of line from A to J which is less than the slope of AE_1. The random error in the model would thus cause the wage rate to change, which means that the wage rate has become endogenous. It may be noted that with the gross average wage rate the problem does not arise in this case, because the gross average wage is AB irrespective of whether the hours worked are H_1 or H_{1+u}. Masters and Garfinkel argued in the quotation above that a net average wage would be preferable to a gross average wage and their reasoning is correct, but *in this case* the gross average wage would be preferable to avoid endogeneity.

This advantage for the gross average wage disappears when overtime premiums are paid and in these circumstances both the gross and net average wage rates suffer from endogeneity bias, as can be explained with reference to Fig. 5.4. The pre-tax budget constraint is ABC (the top of the segment BC is omitted to save space), the post-tax constraint is ADFG and equilibrium is at E_1. The gross average wage rate

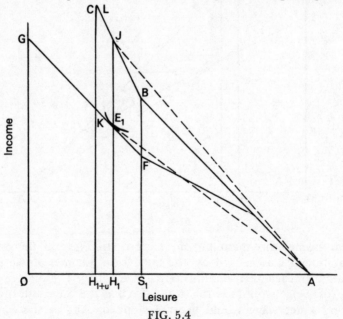

FIG. 5.4

is given by the slope of AJ and net average wage rate by the slope of AE_1. With random error, hours might again be H_{1+u}. This would make the net average wage *rise* to equal the slope of a line connecting A to K. It may be noted in Fig. 5.3, where the budget constraint is concave (to the origin), that endogeneity bias caused the average wage to be inversely related to the error term; while with the convex budget constraint in Fig. 5.4 endogeneity bias is directly related to the error term. With convex budget constraints the gross average wage rate suffers from endogeneity as well as the net average wage. Thus random error causing hours to be H_{1+u} rather than H_1 would mean that the gross average wage would be computed as the slope of a line from A to L, which is greater than the slope of AJ.

The combination of the theoretical indeterminancy of the Type I model and the particularly acute form of endogeneity bias have led to searches for new models without these problems.

Type II studies

The distinguishing feature of what are here called Type II studies is that they employ a linearized budget constraint which solves the theoretical problems outlined above[1] and which reduces endogeneity bias. The way in which the theoretical problem is solved can be illustrated with reference to Fig. 5.5, which is similar to Fig. 5.1 In Fig. 5.5 the after-tax budget constraints of individual 1 (ABFGH) and of individual 2 (ABJK) are reproduced from Fig. 5.1 and the two equilibria are shown as E_1 and E_2. The crucial element in the linearization procedure is to note that E_1 would be the equilibrium position if the budget constraint were Y_1H and E_2 the equilibrium for the budget constraint Y_2K. In the Type II studies a linearized budget constraint is used and frequently the method[2] involves calculating hypothetical intercepts—sometimes termed 'as if' non-employment income,

[1] E. Levin developed a model employing both an average and a marginal wage rate which solved the theoretical problem. This model is discussed in Brown, Levin and Ulph (1974a).

[2] Hall (1973) was the first person to use a linearized budget constraint but

such as Y_1 and Y_2 in Fig. 5.5. Labour supply is then assumed to depend on this hypothetical intercept and on the slope of the linearized budget constraint. Thus individual 1's labour supply is assumed to depend on Y_1 and the slope of the line Y_1H, and 2's labour supply on Y_2 and the slope of Y_2K. This solves the theoretical problem because the two individuals no longer have a common intercept (AB) and a common wage (the slope of BJ = slope of BI in Fig. 5.1), but instead are recognized to have distinct budget constraints which uniquely identify their equilibria.

Type II models also reduce endogeneity bias. Any random error in the model leading to individuals working more or less hours than those indicated will not matter *provided that the individual remains on the same segment of his budget constraint.* The italicized proviso in the last sentence is important. It is the failure of Type II models to deal with this element of the endogeneity problem that has led to the development of Type III models. However before examining the

---

**ACTUAL AND LINEARIZED BUDGET
CONSTRAINTS UNDER A PROGRESSIVE INCOME TAX**

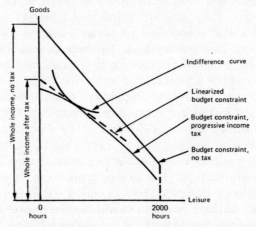

instead of calculating an intercept at zero hours of work, he used a concept which he termed 'whole income after tax', which is in effect an 'as if' intercept calculated at 2,000 hours of work per year. His diagram showing the calculation of whole income is reproduced above. It may be noted that he made allowance for non-linearities associated with progressive tax structures, but not for non-linearities associated with overtime etc.

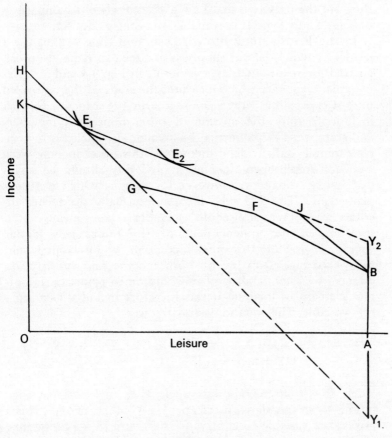

FIG. 5.5

Type III models it is worth looking at some of the results
from the Type II models and to compare results from Type I
and Type II models to examine what difference in the estimates is made by the theoretical and econometric improve-
ments.

Type II results

I propose to report on the findings of two Type II studies :
one American and one British. These two studies are selected
from the relatively small number of Type II studies because

they are the only two that I am aware of where a comparison
of Type I and Type II is available on a single data set.

In the British study Brown, Levin and Ulph (1976) use a
model in which labour supply is assumed to depend on calculated intercepts such as Y_1 and Y_2 in Fig. 5.5 and on a net
marginal wage rate which measures the slope of the linearized
budget constraint. They also use a term 'other income' which
includes mainly the income of other household members
and state transfer payments, but which also includes in principle rental and dividend income. If this other income were
true non-employment income it obviously should be included in the intercept. However for reasons which were explained in Chapter 3 such income, especially the earned income of other household members and means-tested
transfers, is not independent of the individual's labour
supply. To include this other income in the intercept would
thus bias the estimates of both income and substitution
effects. To omit it altogether would be to ignore an important element of income. It was therefore included as a separate variable. The equation estimated was

$$H = a_1 + a_2 MW + a_3 (MW)^2 + a_4 I + a_5 I^2 + a_6 (MW)(I) + a_7 OY + a_8 N + a_9 JS$$

where H = hours worked last week; MW = net marginal wage
rate; I = the calculated intercept; OY = other income; N is a
preference variable to control for need and JS is a preference
variable to control for job satisfaction.

The data was from a specially commissioned survey carried
out from Stirling University in 1971. The population studied
was weekly-paid workers in Great Britain. To be eligible for
inclusion in the equation which is reported here the respondent had to be a married man under 65 who worked at
least eight hours 'last' week and who reported that he was
free to work his desired number of hours (that is, he was not
constrained by demand factors to work an amount different
from the amount he wished to work). He had to come from
a household where either he was the only worker or where
he and his wife alone worked; he had to provide enough
information to allow the variables to be constructed; and he

had to have a positive net marginal wage rate. 'Hours' was defined as 'hours worked in all paid jobs last week'. The marginal wage made appropriate allowances for income taxation, overtime premiums (which varied considerably between individuals) and second jobs. It did not take into account loss of means-tested benefits. The intercept was calculated using hours worked at a previous kink rather than using actual hours of work, in order to eliminate bias in the intercept being associated with measurement error in the dependent variable (see Chapter 3).

The results are given in Table 5.2. It can be seen that the

Table 5.2 *Type II labour supply estimates of British married men*

Marginal wage rate	−24·1*
	(5·18)
Marginal wage rate squared	6·78*
	(2·09)
Intercept	− 1·02*
	(0·150)
Intercept squared	0·00843*
	(0·00211)
Marginal wage rate × intercept	0·624*
	(0·118)
Other income	− 0·189*
	(0·051)
Job satisfaction	0·187*
	(0·045)
Need	0·350*
	(0·07)
Constraint	−
Constant	48·9
N = no. of cases	337
R^2	0·240
R^{-2}	0·222
F	12·9*
Hours	48·2
Price effect	−16·4*
Income effect	− 0·680*
Substitution effect	16·4
Price elasticity	− 0·179
Income elasticity	− 0·011
Substitution elasticity	0·180
Elasticity of substitution	0·247

*Significant at 5 per cent level. (We know of no test of the significance of the substitution effect or of elasticities.)
Standard errors are given below the coefficients.
Source: Brown, Levin and Ulph (1976) Table 1, regression 2B.

Table 5.3 *Comparison of Type I and Type II models*

Variables	Type I	Type II Net marginal wage other income and intercept calculated with actual hours	Type II Net marginal wage other income and intercept calculated with hours at kink
Average wage	−46·18* (20·40)	—	—
Average wage squared	15·20 (4·33)*	—	—
Other income	−0·416 (8·96)	−0·028 (27·0)*	−0·12 (4·89)
Other income squared	0·005 (11·1)	0·005 (12·7)	0·002 (1·82)
Marginal wage	—	−31·66 (19·7)*	−27·05 (39·8)*
Marginal wage squared	—	5·90 (1·44)	9·63 (23·1)*

Intercept	—	0.68 (39.4)*	— 0.608 (15.7)*
Intercept squared	—	0.002 (2.23)	0.004 (1.00)
Average wage times other income	0.246 (1.32)	—	—
Marginal wage times intercept	—	0.232 (2.35)	0.412 (5.13)
Constant	68.29	63.07	59.51
N	505	505	469
R^2	0.18	0.25	0.09
F	22.00	23.10*	6.30*
Price Effect	—28.5	—25.4	—16.1
Income Effect	— 0.22	— 0.56	— 0.37
Substitution Effect	—18.1	+ 0.54	+ 1.3

The numbers in brackets under the coefficients are individual F values.
The significance levels are indicated as follows*, significant at 5 per cent.
Source: Brown, Levin and Ulph (1974).

equation as a whole and all the individual coefficients are significant and that the signs of the income and substitution effects are consistent with theoretical expectations.

Brown, Levin and Ulph have compared the results using Type I and Type II models on their data and the comparison is summarized in Table 5.3.[3] Efforts were made to be as consistent as possible with definitions of variables, numbers of persons, and with functional form. The results from the Type I model on its own look moderately satisfactory until one notices that the substitution effect is negative. It can be seen that the Type II model produces the positive substitution effect expected by theory. The first Type II result shown has the intercept calculated using actual hours of work and it may be noted that there appears to be little difference in the estimate of the price effect. However when the intercept is calculated using hours at the kink to eliminate bias from measurement error in the dependent variable the size of the price effect moves appreciably nearer to zero. It may also be noted that numbers are smaller (reflecting higher data requirements) and that the *apparent* fit and explanatory power of the equation is much reduced.

The approach used by Brown, Levin and Ulph clearly avoids many of the problems of the Type I studies but as they recognized, and as is explained above, the procedure is still endogenous if the random variation in the model results in a change in the segment of the budget constraint.

The other Type II model that I will report on in some detail is an American study by Jonathan Dickinson (1975). Like the Brown, Levin and Ulph study Dickinson's study is of married men (between 25 and 60 in his case) who are free to vary their hours and who have a positive net marginal wage rate. He also uses a calculated intercept (which he terms 'non-wage income, effective level') and a functional form that allows for interactions between the wage rate and the intercept.

There are however many differences in the details of the way the variables are defined: hours are annual hours; in the

[3] The regressions in Tables 5.2 and 5.3 are not directly comparable. The most important difference is that households with workers other than husband or husband and wife only are included in Table 5.3.

version of the model reported here, which is Dickinson's preferred version, the gross marginal wage is defined with a uniform overtime premium of 1·5 times the basic wage rate; the net marginal wage is the gross marginal wage less one minus the marginal tax rate (which is estimated separately).

The intercept is calculated on the assumption that the basic wage rate is paid for the first 2,000 hours per year[4] and overtime wage rate for hours over 2,000. Dickinson proceeds by summing gross non-employment income and the estimated value of gross employment income of both husband and wife. Estimated tax is then substracted from this total and the whole is then brought back to zero hours.

Dickinson tries to minimize the endogeneity problem by splitting his sample into three groups depending on the value of the net marginal wage rate. In his justification for this procedure he notes that the direction of the endogeneity bias depends on whether the kinks are concave or convex. He argues that within each of the bands the bias from overtime premium will roughly cancel out the bias from the change in tax rates.

In his regressions Dickinson employs large numbers of control variables, many of which are interacted with the wage rate and the intercept. As a result there are nearly 30 variables in the regression. Table 5.4 shows the resulting elasticity estimates.

Dickinson's results which are reported here are from his preferred specification. Like Brown, Levin and Ulph he has experimented with Type I models. However Dickinson finds much smaller differences between the alternative specifications than those found by Brown, Levin and Ulph. Dickinson concludes:

Most previous estimates of labour supply functions have thus been based on the assumption of a constant wage rate, at least before taxes, and on the assumption of effective freedom of choice of work hours at that wage rate. In the above comparative exercise we have controlled on the second factor and explored the sensitivity of our estimates to alternative budget specifications. If no wage-income interactions are allowed, the estimates are relatively insensitive to changes

[4] It is assumed that the standard week is 40 hours and that 50 weeks are worked. If either the number of hours or the number of weeks differs then there will be error in the calculations.

Table 5.4 *Estimated labour supply parameters preferred specification[a]*

Wage Rate	Expected Work Hours[b]	Wage Effect	Income Effect	Substitution Effect
White Males, no second job				
under $3.25 ($\bar{w}$ = $2.60)	2307	−109·4 (70·4)	−·101 (·042)	124·7 (107·7)
$3.25–$4.99 ($\bar{w}$ = $4.30)	2183	− 50·5 (36·7)	−·101 (·035)	170·0 (78·9)
$5.00–$9.99 ($\bar{w}$ = $6.10)	2106	− 38·8 (24·6)	−·080 (·033)	130·3 (63·7)
Black Males, no second job				
under $3.25 ($\bar{w}$ = $2.60)	2197	−122·7 (64·2)	−·065 (·052)	20·0 (123·0)
$3.25–$4.99 ($\bar{w}$ = $4.30)	2050	− 63·8 (45·8)	−·065 (·048)	68·4 (92·6)
$5.00–$9.99 ($\bar{w}$ = $6.10)	1949	− 52·1 (43·9)	−·044 (·048)	33·3 (83·6)

[a]Married male workers, no second job, wives not working, select equilibrium sample. Net overtime wage specification, all preference control variables included.

[b]Assumes the following standard characteristics: age 40, 4-9 years on job, 1 week sick time, 190 hours commuting time, children in family, mean values on preference control variables.

Source: Dickinson (1975).

in the marginal wage specification. When this restriction is dropped, however, failure to account for overtime premiums in the wage specification leads to an apparent strengthening of the income effect for low wage workers relative to that for high wage workers. While such a differential is theoretically plausible, the empirical result must be viewed as a consequence of misspecification unless a convincing argument can be made that the effective gross marginal wage rate is closer to the straight time rate than to the overtime rate. (p. 182).

It is not clear why Dickinson's estimates should be much less sensitive to model specification than those of Brown, Levin and Ulph. It is frequently stated that overtime is less common in the US than in the UK and this could be the explanation, were it not for Dickinson's finding that most of his sample (like the UK sample) did not work overtime. The difference might lie in details such as Dickinson assuming a constant overtime premium and a constant number of hours paid at basic rate, while Brown, Levin and Ulph put in separate figures for each individual. It could be simply that various errors in the Type I models happened to cancel out with Dickinson. Brown, Levin and Ulph's findings suggest it would be unwise to assume that this will always happen.

Type III Studies

The major drawback of the Type II studies is that they do not fully solve the endogeneity problem. Type III studies solve the endogeneity problem by estimating each segment of the budget constraint separately and then allowing the individual to choose the budget constraint which gives him the highest utility.

The Type III approach appears to have been evolved quite independently by three separate groups of authors. Ashworth and Ulph (1977a) and Burtless and Hausman (1978) both state they became aware of the work of Wales and Woodland (1979)[5] after they had worked out their own approaches. While it would appear that Wales and Woodland were the first to produce a discussion paper, it is interesting that several people saw more or less the same answer at more or less the same time. Once again there are differences in the detailed approach followed and again it is convenient to choose one study to explain the principles involved. In this case Ashworth and Ulph is taken as the example because it is then possible to compare Type II and III studies on a single body of data.

The Type III procedure can, in principle, be used for budget constraints with any number of linear segments. The budget constraint may be concave throughout, as in Fig. 5.6(a), which could be generated by an income tax with two

---

[5] When in discussion paper form.

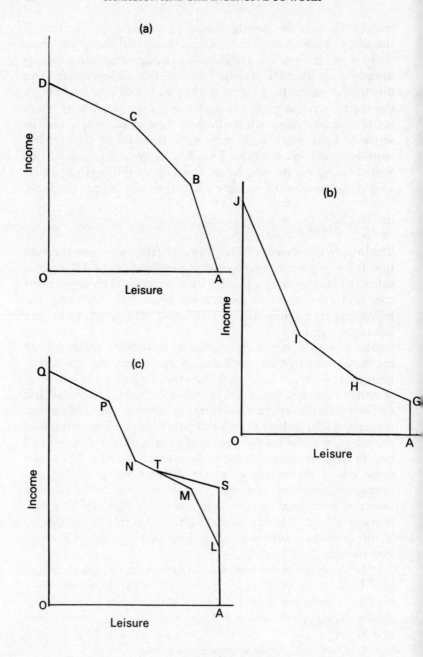

FIG. 5.6

marginal rates. Or the budget constraint could be convex throughout, as in Fig. 5.6(*b*). Such a constraint could arise if there were a means-tested benefit giving GH, an ordinary income tax giving a net wage equal to the slope of HI and an overtime wage rate in the final segment of Fig. 5.6(*b*). Or the constraint could contain alternating convex and concave segments as in Fig. 5.6(*c*). Individuals might be in equilibrium on any of the segments shown. An unconstrained individual would not choose convex points such as H, I or N but might well choose concave points such as B, C, M and P.

In principle, with the Type III procedure all segments of the budget constraint are estimated, but in practice data limitations have usually restricted the analysis to a subset of the segments. An indirect utility function is then employed together with an algorithm that instructs the computer (*a*) to find as many possible equilibria (that is, points of tangency between the utility function and either segments or convex kinks) as it can, and then (*b*) to select from these points on one yielding the highest utility. Clearly the equilibria so chosen will depend on the exact form of the utility function that is employed and it turns out that the results are fairly sensitive to the form of the utility function that is employed.

Ashworth and Ulph use the Stirling data set described earlier. Each individual is assumed to have 4 possible segments to his budget constraint, and a typical case can be represented by Fig. 5.6(*c*). The slopes of these segments can be explained as follows: the slope of LM is the gross wage which is also the net wage rate until the tax threshold is reached; the slope of MN is the gross wage less the basic tax rate; the slope of NP is the slope of net wage for hours in excess of the basic working week; and the slope of PQ is the net wage rate paid in the second job which Ashworth and Ulph assume is always less than the main job wage rate. The first intercept AL is the 'other income' of Brown, Levin and Ulph and the remaining intercepts are 'other income' plus an adjustment factor, to take account of non-linearities in the budget constraint. Because the data requirements of this approach are much greater than those in Type II studies fewer people are analyzed: 335 as against the 434 used in the corresponding Type III study.

Table 5.5. Comparison of Type II and Type III results on Stirling data

Functional Form	(1) Quadratic with separate other income	(2) Quadratic with separate other income	(3) Quadratic with other income in intercept	(4) Quadratic Generalized C.E.S.	(5) C.E.S.
Type II Results					
N	434	339	339	339	339
Price elasticity	−0·107	−0·00130	0·0639	−0·158	−0·507
Income elasticity	−0·016	−0·02	−0·0246	−0·0234	−0·0454
Substitution elasticity	0·204	0·308	0·146	0·249	0·195
Elasticity of substitution	0·274	0·411	0·197	0·352	0·260
Type III Results					
N	—	—	—	339	339
Price elasticity	—	—	—	−0·0650	−0·391
Income elasticity	—	—	—	−0·00371	−0·0462
Substitution elasticity	—	—	—	0·559	0·315
Elasticity of substitution	—	—	—	0·778	0·418

Sources: Ashworth and Ulph (1977a) and Brown, Levin and Ulph (1976).

Table 5.5 contains a selection of Ashworth and Ulph's preliminary results and a comparison with Type II results. The Type III results are given in the bottom of the table. Ashworth and Ulph prefer the results using the generalized C.E.S. utility function because they believe it is a particularly flexible utility function. It can be seen that with this functional form the price elasticity remains a small negative number but it can also be seen that the elasticity of substitution is now very high at nearly 0·8. This is in general in line with the findings of Wales and Woodland that, to use my terminology, Type II studies have underestimated the elasticity of substitution due to their failure to solve completely the endogeneity problem. This is a very important finding with very great potential policy implications. For this reason it is worth looking at the results more closely.

It will be remembered that the extra data requirements of the Type III approach meant that a smaller sample had to be used. Columns 1 and 2 at the top of Table 5.5. show the effect of the change in numbers, where it ·can be seen that elasticity of substitution is higher with the small numbers. This is not implausible, as knowledge of budget constraints and responses to budget constraint changes could well be related. But this may mean that the Ashworth and Ulph results overestimate the true elasticity. A comparison of columns 2 and 3 shows the effect of putting the 'other income' terms into the intercept. It will be remembered from the discussion in Chapter 3 that 'other income' does not correspond to the theoretical construct of non-employment income and it appears that putting this other income into the intercept increases the endogeneity bias in the Type II studies. A comparison of columns 4 and 5 with column 3 shows that the elasticity of substitution is higher with indirect utility functions than with the most comparable quadratic forms. Finally, of course, the comparison of the top and bottom of columns 4 and 5 show the effect of removing the endogeneity problem.

Clearly this is an important advance but there are problems remaining which may be listed. The data requirements restrict numbers. Other income is treated as if it were non-employment income. To date, Ashworth and Ulph have not incorporated preference variables into Type III procedures.

There is a final problem caused by data limitations. Type III studies can in principle handle any number of budget segments but in practice data limitations may restrict the set estimated. The problem may be illustrated with the Ashworth and Ulph study and Fig. 5.6(c). It is very likely that the Ashworth and Ulph procedure will locate some people at M, the kink caused by the tax threshold. However point M may not exist in reality. The reason for this is that people may become eligible for various income maintenance benefits before their income drops below the tax threshold. This is because the tax and social security systems overlap in the UK. However, the Stirling data set does not have very good information on means-tested benefits and, as a result, means-tested benefits have not been modelled by Ashworth and Ulph. These implications are explained with the aid of Fig. 5.7. The budget constraint as modelled by Ashworth and Ulph is ABCDEF and they might find someone at C on I_1. However the true budget constraint with means-tested benefits is AGHDEF and if this had been modelled, equilibrium would have been found at J on I_2. The policy impli-

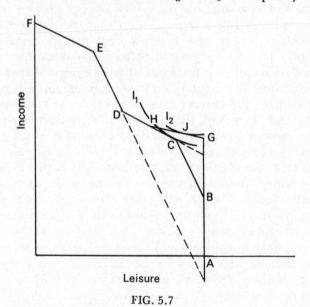

FIG. 5.7

cations of the two positions may be very different. As we saw in Chapter 2 the policy implications of changes in, say, allowances or tax rates for someone at a kink may be very different from those for someone not at a kink and what happens to the kink at C might have no relevance to someone at J.

Conclusions

Clearly there has been considerable progress in the dozen years since Kosters' pioneering work. The present state of evidence suggests strongly that it would be a mistake for policy makers to assume that labour supply is not responsive to tax changes. The evidence suggests that both the people are responsive and that modelling this response very carefully is important. Precisely how responsive people are is still an open question, but it does seem well established that the price elasticity for men is low and negative.

6

THE EXPERIMENTAL APPROACH

The purpose of this chapter is to review the United States' evidence that has been collected in negative income tax (NIT) experiments. There was considerable interest in the 1960s in NIT on both sides of the Atlantic. In the United States one of the main obstacles to adopting NIT was a popular fear that the provision of higher incomes might lead to a very large fall in work. In order to study this and other possible effects, NITs were introduced experimentally in at least five places. The first and best known is the Urban Income Maintenance Experiment (UIME) (better known as the 'New Jersey Experiment'); and others include the Rural (North Carolina and Iowa) Income Maintenance Experiment (RIME), the Gary (Indiana) Income Maintenance Experiment (GIME), the Seattle (Washington) Income Maintenance Experiment (SIME), and the Denver (Colorado) Income Maintenance Experiment (DIME). I discuss results from all five.

The New Jersey Experiment

The New Jersey experiment was carried out at three urban sites in New Jersey (Trenton, Paterson and Passaic, and Jersey City) and one in Pennsylvania (Scranton). To be eligible, a family had to have an able-bodied male between eighteen and fifty-eight who was not in an institution, the armed forces, or full-time education, and to have an income not in excess of 150 per cent of the official poverty line. A total of 1,374 families were enrolled, 724 as experimental families and 650 as controls. The experimental families were allocated to one of eight separate NIT schemes combining four guarantee levels (at 50 per cent, 75 per cent, 100 per cent and 125 per cent of the poverty line) and three tax rates (30 per cent, 50 per cent and 70 per cent). Table 6.1 shows the eight plans chosen and the number assigned to each plan.

The size of the payment received (and hence the extent to which poverty is relieved) of course varied between the

Table 6.1 *New Jersey negative income tax experiment: numbers enrolled and average payment for each plan*

Guarantee level (per cent of poverty line)	Tax rate		
	30%	50%	70%
125	–	N 138	–
		$ 187	
100	–	N 81	N 80
		$ 124	$ 66
75	N 104	N 118	N 84
	$ 104	$ 44	$ 35
50	N 48	N 71	
	$ 46	$ 22	

Notes: N = Number of families.
     $ = Average weekly payment in year 2 of experiment.
Source: Brown (1977).

different experimental groups. Table 6.1 shows the average payment received in each four-week period in the second year of the experiment: 323 families (45 per cent) received more than $25 a week while 321 families (44 per cent) received less than $12 a week. This can be compared with an official poverty line in 1967–68 ranging from $2115 a year ($41 a week) for a two-person family to $5440 a year ($105 a week) for an eight-person family.

The central question of course is what effect these payments, and the accompanying changes in the shape of the budget constraint, had on labour supply. Watts and Horner (1977) found little variation in men's labour supply. They state:

The overall responses to tax rates that (on average) cut net wages in half and to income guarantees that were equal to a substantial fraction of preexperimental income are barely detectable, and could be interpreted as being so minor that further analysis is unwarranted. Further analysis was, however, carried out and tended both to confirm prior hypotheses about the direction of response and to support previous nonexperimental findings of low elasticities of labour supply for prime-age male breadwinners. (p. 58).

Table 6.2 shows the labour supply results for husbands that were estimated from regressions for the middle two years of the experiment using four measures of labour supply. The first three measures (participation, employment and unemployment rates) are clearly not comprehensive. Watts and his associates prefer earnings as the best comprehensive measure of labour supply on the grounds that it includes all three other variables plus any influences the worker may have on his hourly wage rate. The earnings variable, however, may be biased. All families were asked for earnings but it appears that initially some reported net earnings when what the researchers wanted was gross earnings. As experimental families reported income monthly and controls quarterly, Watts and his associates think it is possible that the experimental families learned what was wanted earlier causing a spurious differential in earnings. They thus put most emphasis on hours. Haveman and Watts (1977) summarize the results as follows:

The treatment-control differentials shown for husbands are from regressions in which age, education, number of adults, number and ages of children, sites and pre-program family earnings and labor supply served as control variables . . .
The most striking features of the results for husbands are that all of the differentials are quite small in both absolute and relative terms . . all are statistically insignificant. There are no findings here to indicate a significant reduction in labour supply . . . Moreover, many of the differentials, including all those for blacks, are positive . . . (p. 248)

These results are so surprising that they deserve comment. The results are from regressions that do not include wage rates as independent variables. Other regressions (not reported) do control 'for normal wages and normal income as a fraction of the poverty level, and that permit non-linear wage effects . . . These regressions do little better than the first set in disclosing significant effects of the treatment.' (Rees and Watts (1975), pp. 78-9.)

The results from the New Jersey experiment have been re-analyzed by several authors. Robert Hall (1975) has argued that the results for whites do in fact show a significant reduction in hours for white husbands. Hall's data are reproduced in Table 6.3. Hall compares hours of the experimental group before and during the experiment, which sug-

Table 6.2 *Basic experimental differentials for husbands: New Jersey experiment*

	Quarters	Labour force participation (percentage)	Employment (percentage)	Unemployment (percentage)	Hours per week	Earnings per week (Dollars)
All	1–4	1·8	0·2	1·6	−0·91	2·51
	5–8	−1·2	−3·0	1·8	−1·97	−0·02
	9–12	−0·7	−4·4	3·7	−3·46**	−3·84
	3–10	−0·4	−2·5	2·1	−2·07	−0·08
Black	1–4	−0·9	2·5	−3·4	1·86	6·93
	5–8	0·1	−0·3	0·4	0·54	8·10
	9–12	−1·1	1·1	0·0	1·00	8·01
	3–10	0·1	1·1	−1·0	0·93	8·29*
Spanish-speaking	1–4	−0·5	−6·9**	6·4	−3·87*	2·64
	5–8	−1·0	4·1	3·1	−1·20	2·23
	9–12	−0·1	−1·0	0·9	0·95	6·93
	3–10	−0·9	−4·0	3·1	−0·98	4·48

Note: Control variables include age, education, preenrollment hours, weeks worked in year before experiment, site, and family size.
Regressions estimated 15 parameters (14 for Spanish-speakers) including experimental differential.
15 parameters (14 for Spanish-speakers) including experimental differential.
* Significant at the 10 per cent level.
** Significant at the 5 per cent level.
Source: Watts and Horner (1977), p. 61.

Table 6.3 *Hours worked by husbands*
in New Jersey experiment

	Experimental group	Control group	Difference
White			
Before experiment	34·1	34·8	
During experiment	31·8	34·4	−2·6
Difference	− 2·3	− 0·4	
Black			
Before experiment	31·8	31·9	
During experiment	31·2	28·5	+2·7
Difference	− 0·6	− 3·4	
Spanish-speaking			
Before experiment	32·9	36·7	
During experiment	31·7	32·9	−1·2
Difference	− 1·2	− 3·8	

Source: Hall (1975).

gests that the experiment reduced work by 2.3 hours per
worker per week. A comparison of hours worked by the
experimental and control groups during the experiment
suggests a reduction in work of 2.6 hours. These measures
(plus another two) all show a significant reduction in hours
for the experimental group. It is clearly important that someone should attempt to account for the differences between
Hall's results and those of Watts.

Hall's figures for black and Spanish-speaking families show
relatively little change in hours for the experimental families
and large reductions in hours for the controls, and the
results for blacks seem to confirm the 'wrong' sign found by
Watts. However, Hall dismisses the data for non-white as
unreliable on the ground that the attrition rate is so high.
Hall gives data, reproduced in Table 6.4, 'on the percentages
of families lacking continuous structure and data throughout
the experimental period'.

John F. Cogan (1978) has also reanalysed the New Jersey
data and has concluded that the experiment caused a much

Table 6.4 *Percentages of families lacking continuous data and structures: New Jersey experiment*

	Experimental group	Control group
	%	%
White	22	34
Black	46	45
Spanish-speaking	56	61
Total	41	45

Source: Hall (1975).

larger reduction in hours worked than the original findings. His results are dependent on splitting the sample between those who participated in the negative income tax programme and those who did not. Not surprisingly those who participated in the programme reduced their labour supply by much more than those who did not. The big question is whether this splitting of the sample is reasonable. Cogan states: 'There is no evidence of simultaneity (in the statistical sense) between NIT program participation and hours of work' (p. 23). On the other hand it could be argued that much of the expected effects of a NIT would be captured in the decision about whether to participate in the programme.

The Rural Income Maintenance Experiment

As the New Jersey experiment was conducted entirely in urban areas it was thought that its findings might not be applicable to rural areas. The rural experiment was carried out on locations in Iowa and North Carolina. The experimental design was similar to that used in the New Jersey experiment. The sample was divided between wage earners and farmers and the results summarized here refer only to the wage earners. Included in the experiment were 269 husband and wife families with wages as the primary source of income, where the couple were married throughout and where the husband was under 63 years of age, and not disabled. 146 families were treated as controls and 118 were assigned to

1 of 5 experimental plans according to the plan in Table 6.5. The labour supply results are summarized in Table 6.6. The overall labour supply reduction was 13 per cent with a much larger reduction by wives and other dependents than by husbands.

Table 6.5 *Percentage distribution of experimental wage-earner families among experimental plans: rural experiment*

Basic benefit as percent of poverty line	Implicit tax rate		
	30%	50%	70%
50		4	
75	31	34	6
100		25	

Source: Rural Income Maintenance Experiment (1976), p. 13.

The Gary Income Maintenance Experiment

The Gary (Indiana) Income Maintenance Experiment was designed to test the impact of four NIT plans on a black urban sample which contained many workers receiving social security payments (AFDC) prior to the experiment and many families with female heads. The Gary labour market was also very highly structured which may have made adjustments in hours difficult. Table 6.7 shows the distribution of the sample between families with and without husbands present for both controls and the four experimental plans.

The labour supply responses for households with both husbands and wives present is given in Table 6.8. It should be noted that these families were typically not very poor and were eligible for only modest amounts of NIT payments on average at their initial hours of work. The total reduction in husbands' hours of about 7 per cent was largely caused by a small number of individuals leaving the labour force rather than by a small reduction in hours on the part of a larger number of individuals. This may reflect the institutional

Table 6.6 *Weighted experimental responses for selected measures of income and wage work: Rural experiment*

| | Control/Experimental Differential as Percent of Control Mean[a] | | | |
	N. Carolina Blacks	N. Carolina Whites	Iowa	Eight-State[b] Aggregate
Families				
Total income	−14	− 9	−18	−13
Wage income	−14	− 8	−17	−12
Wage hours	−10	−18	− 5	−13
Number of earners	− 6	−16	− 8	−11
Husbands				
Wage income	− 7	0	−10	− 4
Wage hours	− 8	+ 3	− 1	− 1
If employed	− 1	− 1	0	− 1
Wives				
Wage income	−41	− 3	−32	−25
Wage hours	−31	−23	−22	−27
If employed	−25	−28	−38	−28
Dependents				
Wage income	−19	−57	− 8	−39
Wage hours	−16	−66	−27	−46

[a]Responses standardized to a 45% tax/80% basic benefit plan.

[b]Weighted averages of the basic data from which the subsample percentages were derived, using the following weights: NC-B, ·31788; NC-W, ·48943; Ia., ·19269.

Source: Rural Income Maintenance Experiment, (1976), p. 38.

rigidity referred to above. The 17 per cent reduction in hours (which was only about one hour a week) was due almost equally to wives leaving the labour force and to reduction in hours by those remaining at work.

Table 6.9 shows the labour supply responses of female-headed families. These families were typically much poorer than families with both husband and wife present. Only 10 per cent of husband/wife families were below the official poverty line. In contrast 38 per cent of female-headed families not eligible for AFDC were below the poverty line and 74 per cent of female-headed families who were eligible for AFDC were also below the poverty line. It may be noted that none of the changes in the tables is statistically significant and that the non-AFDC families' hours of work increased.

Burtless and Hausman (1978) have also analyzed the Gary data. They have used a Type III study in which they have made use of Roy's identity to construct an indirect utility function based on a labour supply with constant elasticity of substitution. They have tested for truncation bias in the sample selection, which in this case extended to 2·4 times the poverty line, and have found none. Their results are given in Table 6.10 where it can be seen that their wage elasticity (what has been called price elasticity here) is effectively zero. This means that the Gary population would have only a small difference in their response to differing tax rates in NIT programmes, as can be seen from Fig. 6.1. In the absence of an NIT the budget con-

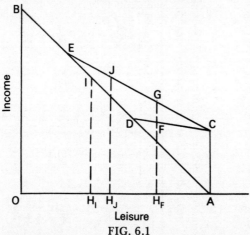

FIG. 6.1

straint is AB. With an NIT providing a guaranteed income of AC, the budget constraint would be ACDB or ACEB depending on whether a high or low tax rate were chosen. If the high tax rate equilibrium were at F, working AH_F hours, the zero price elasticity implies that the person would be at G if the tax rate were lower where he would still work AH_F hours. However, it may be noted that someone at I working AH_J hours with the high tax rate would

Table 6.7 *Analysis sample for the initial findings report:*
number of families by NIT status, income and family composition: Gary Experiment

| Support level: implicit tax rate: | Experimental families | | | | | Control families | All families |
| | Poverty Level | | .75 Poverty Level | | All experimental families | | |
	40%	60%	40%	60%			
Families with husband present							
Income:							
Less than half the poverty line	3	2	2	3	10	3	13
Less than the poverty line but greater than half	6	7	3	4	20	2	22
More than the poverty line but less than 1·5	11	10	10	18	49	47	96
Above 1·5 of the poverty line	28	29	47	25	129	77	206
Total	48	48	62	50	208	129	337

Families with husband absent

Income:

Less than half the poverty line	36	29	57	24	146	111	257
Less than the poverty line but greater than half	15	13	31	12	71	94	165
More than the poverty line but less than 1·5	11	10	7	62	90	26	116
Above 1·5 of the poverty line	16	15	18	16	65	27	92
Total	78	67	113	114	372	258	630
All Families	126	115	175	164	580	387	967

Source: Kehrer (1977), p. 47.

Table 6.8 *Estimates of work disincentives for husbands and wives participating in the Gary Income Maintenance Experiment: end of the second year*

	Husbands			Wives		
	Range of response[a]	Control mean	Percent of control mean	Range of response[a]	Control mean	Percent of control mean
For the whole sample						
Disincentive effect on:						
Hours worked per week	— 2·5	36·0	—7	— 1·0	5·7	—17
Labour force participation	—06 to —07*	·96	—6 to —7	·04 to —001	·17	+24 to 0
Employment	—05 to —08*	·89	—6 to —9	·01 to —03	·16	— 6 to —19
For those employed prior to the experiment	—06	·98	—6	—·20*	·77	—26
For those not employed prior to the experiment	—26*	·60	43	·02	·07	—29
For those who were employed at the end of the second year						
Disincentive effect on:						
Hours worked per week	—7	40·4	— 2	— 5·7 to —4·7	35·5	—16 to —13
Earnings per week	$— 17·19*	$160·95	—11	n.a.		

[a] Responses were estimated using two alternative techniques to control for preenrollment differences in work effort between the experimental and control groups. Where different estimates were obtained from the two techniques, both estimates are reported. The first estimate was calculated with the technique that subtracted preenrollment differences from the differences in work effort observed at the end of the second year. The second estimate was calculated using the technique that controlled for preexperimental work effort in calculating the disincentive effect. See the discussion of Study Methodology, above.

*Significant at the ·10 level of statistical confidence.

n.a. = not available.

Source: Kehrer (1977), p. 56.

Table 6.9 *Estimates of work disincentives for female heads of families participating in the Gary Income Maintenance Experiment by preexperiment AFDC status: end of the second year*

	AFDC			Non-AFDC		
	Range of Response[a]	Control mean	Percent of control mean	Range of Response[a]	Control mean	Percent of control mean
For the whole sample						
Disincentive effect on:						
Hours worked per week	−3	6·5	−5	·3	14·7	+2
Employment	·002 to −·04	·18	+1 to −22	·04 to ·001	·41	+10 to 0
For those employed prior to the experiment	−·11	·65	−17	·06	·62	+10
For those not employed prior to the experiment	−·03	·09	−33	−·03	·25	−12
For those who were employed at the end of the second year						
Disincentive effect on:						
Hours worked per week	3·5 to 2·4	35·9	+10 to +7	−2·9 to 1·3	35·9	−8 to +4
Earnings per week	$5-11	$86·90	+6	−6·04	$86·93	−7

Note: None of the estimates of work effort response in this table are large enough to have occurred through chance.

[a] Responses were estimated using two alternative techniques to control for preenrollment differences in work effort between the experimental and control groups. Where different estimates were obtained from the two techniques, both estimates are reported. The first estimate was calculated with the technique that substracted preenrollment differences from the differences in work effort observed at the end of the second year. The second estimate was calculated using the technique that controlled for preexperimental work effort in estimating the disincentive effect. (See the section on Study Methodology.)

Source: Kehrer (1977), p. 70.

Table 6.10 *Estimates of labour supply and indirect utility function: Gary Experiment*

Variable	Parameter Estimates
Constant	3·75043
	(·02555)
Primary Education	·01078
	(·00558)
Adults (N)	·03300
	(·01272)
Poor health	—·02224
	(·00438)
Age	—·00869
	(·01347)
Wage elasticity, $\bar{a}$	·00003
	(·01632)
Mean income elasticity, β	—·04768
	(·00465)
Variance of β distribution, σ_1^2	·06751
	(·00399)
Variance of ϵ_{2i}, σ_2^2	·00135
	(·00022)

Note: Observations (N) = 380; log of the likelihood function = $- 196 \cdot 27$. Asymptotic standard errors in parentheses.
Sources: Burtless and Hausman (1978).

reduce his hours to AH_J if the tax rate were lowered. While the price elasticity in Table 6.10 is zero the income elasticity is significantly negative.

The Seattle and Denver Experiments

The Seattle and Denver experiments provided for three levels of guaranteed income (in 1971 dollars): $3800, $4800 and $5600, and four tax rates. (Keeley *et al* (1977, 1978). One of the features of the Seattle and Denver experiments has been to experiment with non-linear tax rates. Thus, while two of the tax rates employed were constant at 50 and 70 per cent, two of the rates declined by an average of 25 per cent for each £1,000 rise in income. The starting tax for these declining programmes was 70 and 80 per cent.

The researchers estimated the effects of the experiment by comparing hours worked in the year prior to the experiment with hours worked in the second year of the experiment. The income effect was estimated as the effect on hours of a change in disposable income at pre-experimental hours and the substitution effect as the effect on hours of a change in the net wage rate as a result of the experiment. For non-workers the wage rate was estimated from the wage rate of workers. This may lead to biased estimates (see Chapter 7) but Keeley *et al* (1978) argue that the bias may be small because they have used a net wage, rather than a gross wage, for the substitution effect. The estimates of income and substitution effects at the means of the independent variables are given in Table 6.11, for that proportion of the sample who were workers and who were below the break-even levels of income. It should be noted that these results are the combined results from all of the NIT programmes. These responses are quite large as they imply a total reduction in hours of 5·3 per cent for husbands, 22·0 per cent for wives, and 11·2 per cent for female heads.

One of the problems with the experimental approach is that experiments have a finite time horizon: three years in the case of the New Jersey experiment. This raises the question of whether one can reasonably infer what would happen with a permanent NIT from a three-year experiment. In order to test for this time factor at least in part, some of those enrolled in the Seattle and Denver projects were enrolled for three years while others were enrolled for five years. There were no significant differences in the labour

Table 6.11 *Substitution and income effects at the mean (Estimated asymptotic standard errors in parentheses)*

	Husbands	Wives	Female heads
Substitution effect at the mean $(\hat{b}_s \, \Delta \bar{w})$	− 55·7 (24·9)	−63·8 (34·7)	− 59·1 (31·0)
Income effect at the mean $[\hat{b}_4 \, \Delta Y_d(H_p)]$	− 47·1 (37·4)	−198·6 (61·7)	−117·3 (45·7)
Total effect at the mean	−102·8 (33·0)	−262·4 (55·1)	−176·4 (43·6)
Mean hours of work in preexperimental period $(\bar{H}p)$	1,922	1,194	1,577

Source: Keeley *et al* (1978)

supply responses between the two groups in the second year of the experiment. There was no statistically-significant evidence of differences between the labour supply responses of blacks and whites or between the two cities.

It seems reasonable to conclude on the basis of the further evidence now available that the initial results from the New Jersey experiment can be regarded as an exception and that NIT do cause significant reductions in labour supply as predicted by the theory.

7

CROSS SECTION ECONOMETRIC STUDIES ON WOMEN

This chapter contains a brief discussion of econometric work on the labour supply decisions of women, that is based on the individual model outlined in earlier chapters. The principal differences that require discussion arise from the fact that many women, particularly married women, do not undertake market work, and that women who do market work typically work fewer hours than men. It will be possible to keep the discussion brief for three reasons. (1) Only a sample of results will be reported; (2) no attempt will be made to repeat the argument of earlier chapters where there are no important differences between the treatment of men and women; (3) it seems particularly important to treat married women's labour supply decisions in a household context—the subject matter of the next chapter.

The basic model of labour supply assumes that everyone has a positive marginal wage rate. This can be observed for workers who are paid by the hour but it cannot be directly observed for people who do not work. This is in principle a problem for both men and women but in practice the problem is much more severe for women—particularly married women. One approach to this problem is to estimate a predicted wage for non-working women based on demographic characteristics such as age, education, working experience, etc. The wage is predicted from the sample of workers and then assigned to non-workers. However, this procedure can lead to biased estimates, as Gronau (1973) and Heckman (1974) have shown. The market wage is what would be predicted from such an exercise. This is the amount employers would be willing to pay (Heckman calls it the offered wage). However if someone is voluntarily not working it is presumably because their supply price (Heckman's asking wage) is above the offered wage. Heckman has developed the following procedure. He estimates both offered wage (ow) and the asking wage (aw). The offered wage is assumed to

depend on the workers' skill. Specifically Heckman assumes
the offered wage will be a positive function of both education and labour experience. It is assumed that the offered
wage is the same for every hour that is worked. The asking
wage is assumed to depend on the wife's hours of work, the
husband's wage, the prices of goods, non-employment income and a vector of other factors representing household
technology, number of children, etc. The assumption that
the wife's asking wage depends on her hours of work is critical to the analysis, as is the further assumption that the
asking wage is a monotonically-increasing function of hours
worked. If a woman has an asking wage everywhere above the
offered wage, she doesn't work. However if at zero hours of
work the offered wage is above the market wage the woman
will wish to work to the point where the average wage equals
the market wage. The argument is illustrated in Fig. 7.1,
where OA is the endowment of hours, AB non-employment
income, the offered wage (ow) is represented by the slope
of BC, and the monotonically-increasing average wage is
represented by DE which rises to the left as hours of work
increase. If DE lies everywhere above BC, as in part (a), zero
hours are worked. However if BC lies above DE at zero hours
of work, as in part (b), the woman will adjust hours of work
to equate BC with DE which means that equilibrium hours
occur at AH hours.

Heckman's results are given in Table 7.1 for the case when
labour supply is measured in annual hours. The upper part
of the table refers to his whole sample of white wives aged
30 to 44, while the lower part includes working wives only.
From the upper part of the table it can be seen that a child
under six raises the asking wage by 18 per cent. It can also
be seen that the asking wage is a positive function of net
assets, the husband's wage and, in confirmation of the model,
of labour supply. It may be noted that education raises the
offered wage more than the asking wage, implying that extra
education will increase both participation rates and hours
worked for participants. The effects on the subsample of
working women shown at the bottom of the table are rather
different. In particular it may be noted that for the working
subsample the effect of children on the asking wage is much

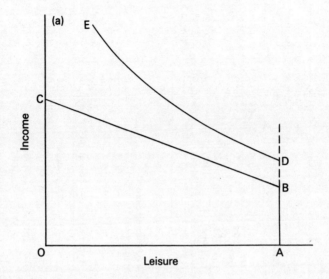

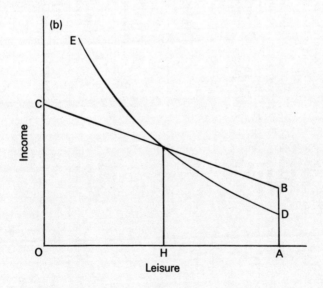

FIG. 7.1

Table 7.1 *Estimates of the asking wage and the offered wage*

Annual hours worked[a]

	Intercept	Number of children less than six	Net assets	Wage rate of husband	Experience	Education	Labour supply	Standard deviation
ln asking wage	—·623 (·088)	·179 (.019)	$\cdot 135 \times 10^{-5}$ ($\cdot 055 \times 10^{-5}$)	·051 (·007)	—	·0534 (·007)	$\cdot 63 \times 10^{-3}$ ($\cdot 05 \times 10^{-3}$)	·532 (·019)
ln offered wage	—·982 (·11)	—	—	—	·048 (·004)	·0761 (·0075)	—	·452 (·0121)

The estimated correlation of disturbances across equations is ·6541 (·046)

Annual hours worked: full information maximum likelihood applied to the subsample of working women[a]

	Intercept	Number of children less than six	Net assets	Wage rate of husband	Experience	Education	Labour supply	Standard deviation
ln asking wage	—1·28 (·18)	·0703 (·09)	$\cdot 169 \times 10^{-5}$ ($\cdot 78 \times 10^{-6}$)	·0376 (·01)	—	·0623 (·008)	$\cdot 83 \times 10^{-3}$ ($\cdot 95 \times 10^{-4}$)	·469 (·012)
ln offered wage	— ·36 (·086)	—	—	—	·0195 (·0025)	·0681 (·007)	—	·507 (·035)

The estimated correlation of disturbances across equations is ·591 (·09)

[a]Asymptotic standard errors in parentheses.

Source: Heckman (1974).

less; that there is no longer any difference in the effects of education as between the two wage rates; and that experience seems less important as a determinant of the market wage. The results in the upper part of the table are preferable theoretically and the differences are large enough to suggest that the proposed method is important. Heckman does not provide a great deal of information about the implication of his results for labour supply estimates but he does suggest that a 10 per cent increase in the real wage would increase labour supply by 160 hours a year.

One way of sidestepping the problems caused by non-working wives is to omit them from the sample! Clearly this procedure has a high cost: for example, if one wanted to know the effect of a tax change on hours supplied the estimates would at best[1] show the effect on workers. It is conceivable that the effects of the policy change on workers would be swamped if tax changes caused a substantial change in participation rates.

Another important 'institutional' feature of women's labour supply is that they seldom work overtime. This means that if the social security system is ignored, budget constraints are concave to the origin, for the majority of women. It seems likely that this concavity will eliminate the problem of theoretical indeterminancy for women discussed above (see Chapter 2). It is also likely to affect the nature of the endogeneity problem. The nature of this effect will depend on the definition of the wage rate.

We can best explore this problem by looking at two recent British studies. It greatly simplifies the exposition of the problem if we assume that there are only two segments of the budget constraint for British women[2]. Thus in Fig. 7.2 there is AB of net non-employment income, a gross average wage rate (gaw), a tax exemption level of OX, a tax rate t for income above the exemption level which means that for

---

[1] The elimination of those with zero hours can cause truncation bias.

[2] Strictly this would only be true if no women had social security receipts, or overtime, or second jobs, or faced higher tax rates because of high earnings of themselves and/or their husbands. Greenhalgh has estimated that the 'great majority' of women meet this criterion.

incomes above OX the net marginal wage (nmw) is given
by the slope of DF.

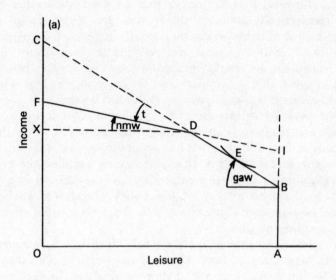

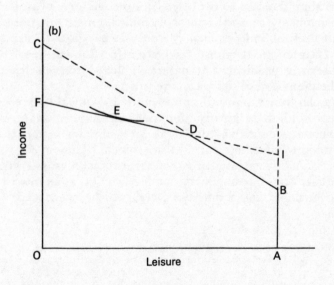

FIG. 7.2

The first study to be looked at is that of Greenhalgh (1979). In terms of the classification system used in Chapter 5 her study is a Type I study: that is to say she assumes that labour supply depends on net non-employment income AB and the gross average wage rate (the slope of BDC). However, the particular formulation she employs avoids two of the problems usually associated with Type I models, although Mrs. Greenhalgh does not draw attention to this. Because budget constraints are (almost) always concave the problem of theoretical indeterminancy does not arise. Furthermore the problem of endogeneity does not arise for someone who remains on the same segment of their budget constraint, because any change in hours and income associated with the random error of the model will not affect the gross average wage rate. However random error causing movement from one segment of the budget constraint to the other will cause endogeneity bias. The problem can be seen from Fig. 7.2. In part (a) where the worker's income is below the tax threshold the model correctly uses non-employment income AB and the gross average wage. In part (b), where tax is paid, the marginal wage rate is given by the slope of DF, while the wage that is used in the regressions is the slope of BDC. Similarly the non-employment income term AB should have been adjusted (to AI) to incorporate the value of the tax allowance. Mrs Greenhalgh has an extended discussion of the problem, in which she recognizes the bias but argues that it is likely to be small 'since the omitted dichotomous variable [taxpayer, non taxpayer] is not closely correlated in a linear fashion with the included variables'. She further argues that 'it will be reduced by large amounts of exogenous variation due to the family income and taste variables, since the shift will occur at different wages for these various types of individual, thus helping to randomise with respect to W the contribution of the omitted variable to the error on the equation '(p. 9). With Mrs Greenhalgh's data set it is not possible to use the more sophisticated techniques which can test for endogeneity bias. Nevertheless there are reasons why one might expect endogeneity bias to be more serious for women than for men. The first is that the budget constraint is concave, which means that all of the bias will work in the same direction. (In contrast, if overtime were regularly worked there would be a convex kink which would cancel out at least some of the bias). In addition, in the Stirling study it appeared that a number of women worked to about the income level of the tax threshold which makes it more likely that random error will cause a movement to a different segment of the constraint.

Other problems with this study are: it includes people who do not have a positive marginal wage rate, and it uses a predicted wage rate, which has the advantage of not causing bias from measurement error in hours. However the predicted wage gives rise to other problems. Also, because the wage rate is predicted using a sample that contains people that do not have a positive marginal wage, the estimates of the wage rate for those with a positive wage may be biased. For example people with high educational qualifications are more likely to enter professions that have *high earnings* but a *zero marginal wage rate*. A wage rate equation explains

$$\text{the average wage} = \frac{\text{income}}{\text{hours}}.$$

While one can understand why education can lead to higher earnings in management and the professions, there is no reason to expect such earnings, when divided by hours, to explain hours. Other problems with a predicted wage have been explained by Killingsworth (1975) as follows:

the sort of regression used in most studies to obtain the 'predicted' wage in fact accounts for rather little of the total variation in wages, so that the use of 'imputed' wage not only suppresses a good deal of the variation observed in actual wages but also in effect assigns the same wage to all persons with the same values for the 'predictor' variables (even though they may have very different values for variables which influence wages—hours of work, experience, quality of education, etc.—but are not used as 'predictors'. In addition, it is possible that 'predictors' such as age and education affect supply not only via the wage but also in other, more direct, ways by, for example, altering (or in effect measuring) tastes, non-pecuniary factors, etc. (p.77)

A further difficulty is that Mrs Greenhalgh uses a functional form in which it is assumed that both non-employment income and the wage rate[3] have a linear effect on hours. The effect of this is to preclude the possibility of a quadratic labour supply function of, for example, the backward bending type. Quadratic equations were estimated (but not reported) which did suggest the labour supply was backward bending at higher wage rates. The results reported here relate to working women only. She found a *gross* wage elasticity of 0·717 (it should be noted that this is not a price elasticity), an income elasticity of −0·221, and a substitution elasticity of 0·795.

In another study of British women, McGlone and Ruffell (1978) employ a Type II model such as is illustrated in Fig. 7.2. For non-taxpayers the intercept is non-employment income (AB in part (*A*)) and the wage is the slope of BD. For taxpayers the intercept is AI and the marginal wage is given by the slope of DF. They employ a quadratic functional form. Like the standard Type II models discussed for men, the model is correctly specified theoretically, does not suffer from bias due to measurement error in hours, does not suffer from endogeneity bias for people who remain on the same segment of their budget constraint, but *does* suffer from endogeneity bias when random error moves people to a different segment of their budget constraints. This is recognized by McGlone and Ruffell who speculate—for reasons given above—that it may be serious. However, their object is to explore a different problem—the treatment of preferences. It may well be the case that preferences are particularly important for married women because of their traditional role in child-rearing and home-making. This is a difficult area because theory gives very little guide, as can be made clear by considering the example of children. It seems fairly obvious that children will have two opposing effects on labour supply. Their physical needs have to be provided for, which requires both extra money (that is, more work), and extra time at home (that is, less work). Given the almost total dependence of very young children and the traditional role of women, it is easy to predict that women with very young children will work less. However, that is not enough to tell

[3] In some equations the average wage is used, while in others the logarithm of the average wage is used.

us how the supply curves of women with children compare
with those of women without children.

The point is illustrated in Fig. 7.3, where *assumed* supply
curves for women without children are shown as solid lines

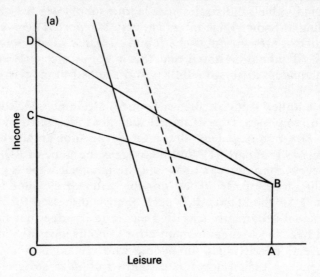

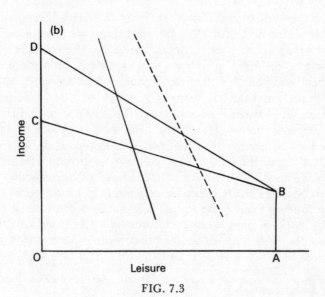

FIG. 7.3

and supply curves of women with children are shown as dashed lines. It is assumed in both parts of the diagram that women with children work less than women without children. In part (a) it is assumed that the effect of children in reducing labour suppy is the same at all wage rates. In part (b) it is assumed that low-wage women with children reduce their labour supply by more than high-wage women relative to women without children (perhaps because high-wage women can afford to pay someone to care for their children). Clearly there are many possibilities in principle but the important point is to have econometric techniques that could distinguish between A and B should such a distinction exist in the real world.

The standard econometric technique of putting in control variables (for example, a dummy variable to represent the presence of pre-school-age children) fails to capture this possibility, as it would show some average reduction in supply.

McGlone and Ruffell (1978) emphasize in their paper that they have not solved the endogeneity problem and speculate that it may be serious. This speculation is confirmed in Ruffell (1979) and for that reason the McGlone and Ruffell (1978) results are largely of methodological interest and therefore are not reported. Ruffell (1979) uses a Type III technique to explore the endogeneity problem, in which he estimates the supply function directly (rather than employing indirect utility functions as employed by Wales and Woodland and other writers).

With multi-segment budget constraints it is likely that some individuals will be in 'equilibrium' at concave kinks in their budget constraints. The wage rate is not defined at such points and Ruffell experiments with three definitions of the wage rate: the slope of the budget constraint below the kink, the slope of the budget constraint above the kink and the average slope. Ruffell's results are sensitive to the definition adopted and he argues that the average slope is to be preferred. It also seems likely on the basis of other evidence that the results are sensitive to the way in which the income of other household members is treated in the intercept.

Ruffell's results are given in Table 7.2. To be eligible the

Table 7.2 *Labour supply elasticities for British women*

	Type II Model	Type III Model
Price	—0·00	0·72
	(0·09)	(0·03)
Income	—0·11	—0·16
	(0·09)	(0·03)
Substitution	0·04	0·77
	(0·09)	(0·03)
Of substitution	0·02	0·35
	(0·04)	(0·01)

(Standard errors are given in brackets.)
Source: Ruffell (1979).

women had to be under retirement age, not ill, from a house-hold where there was no other worker except her husband, not on bonus, free to vary hours in at least one direction and to provide the information necessary to estimate the model. These criteria eliminated all but 129 of the 505 women in the Stirling sample. It is clear from the table that the Type II model, which does not solve the endogeneity problem, results in a large bias and this is confirmed by Ashworth and Ulph's (1977a) results for women.

Most of the available evidence suggests that women's labour supply is much more responsive than that of men and that the price elasticity is a relatively large positive number. There are, however, several reasons why existing elasticities' estimates may be less firmly based for women than for men. (1) Most studies do not adequately deal with non-workers. (2) Endogeneity bias appears to be more acute for women than for men. (3) It seems particularly important to consider women in the context of household models. (4) Given the traditional role of women, modelling their preferences accurately may be especially important. While there are studies that can be said to tackle each of these problems in-dividually there is no study that tackles them all. There is evidence that the elasticities are sensitive to each of the problems mentioned. It would be unwise to infer from exist-ing estimates what the elasticities would be if all of the problems were solved simultaneously.

8
HOUSEHOLD MODELS

The models discussed thus far all suffer from the obvious limitation that they do not allow fully for the possibility of interaction between the labour supply decisions of different household members. Many individual models allow for a one-way effect by including the net employment income of other members in the intercept of the individual being examined. For example in studies of married women the wife's labour supply may be assumed to depend on her wage, the true net non-employment income of the household, and her husband's net employment income. When the husband's net employment income is included in the intercept there is the assumption that this will affect the wife's labour supply in the same way that it would be affected by true non-employment income; that is, an increase in the husband's wage rate which increases his income will necessarily decrease the wife's labour supply (if income and leisure are normal goods). Because individual models do not allow for the possibility that the wife's labour supply decisions also influence the husband's decision these models are sometimes referred to as 'male chauvinist models'.

There are two principal ways in which the joint labour supply decision has been approached in the literature. In both approaches it is assumed that households have a common budget constraint which depends on household non-employment income and the wage rates of both workers[1] which in principle (but not always in practice) are suitably modified for non-linearities introduced by the tax and social security systems, overtime premiums etc. Where the two approaches differ is in their assumptions about utility functions. One possibility is that husband and wife try to maximize a single preference function which depends on their joint consumption of goods plus the leisure of the husband

[1] The literature is almost entirely confined to husband-and-wife households, which neglects the possibility that either two-or-more-adult households may budget jointly and/or make joint labour supply decisions.

and of the wife. These models are usually referred to as neo-classical models although Killingsworth (1976) proposes the more descriptive term 'family-budget constraint-family utility model'.

In addition to the standard price, income, and substitution effects which measure the response of an individual's labour supply to a change in his own wage, the neo-classical model has corresponding measures for the effect of the wage of one member of the household on the labour supply of the other member of the household. A distinguishing feature of this model is that while the sign of the cross-substitution effect is indeterminate, the magnitude is the same for both workers. Thus if family utility is held constant an increase in the hus-band's (wife's) wage might either increase or decrease labour of the wife (husband), but the effect of a change in the hus-band's wage on the wife's labour supply should be the same as the wife's wage on the husband's labour supply. Few empirical studies have found that this condition holds (ex-ceptions are Rosen (1978), Wales and Woodland (1976), and Wales and Woodland (1977).

This is one reason why other models have been explored. The most widely used alternative is the Leuthold model (see Leuthold 1968) in which there is a family budget con-straint, but which provides for separate utility functions for husband and for wife. Killingsworth terms this model 'the individual utility-family budget constraint model'. Utility for each worker depends on household consumption and on individual leisure. The most important difference between the Leuthold and neo-classical model is that in the Leuthold model there is no requirement that cross-substitution effects be equal — in fact there are no cross-substitution effects *per se*. If the husband has an increase in his wage rate, family income will rise, which will have an income effect on the wife. In addition there is a further effect, which Killingsworth calls the indirect income effect, associated with the husband's substitution effect. The substitution effect will cause the husband to work more and hence raise family income further. This further increase in family income will reduce the wife's labour supply further. While the cross-substitution effect in the neo-classical model can be either positive or negative, the indirect income effect is necessarily negative (if leisure is a normal good), but there is no requirement that the indirect income effect of husband and wife should be equal.

It may of course be the case that some families behave in the way the neo-classical model predicts while others may behave in the way the Leuthold model predicts.[2] Nevertheless it is an interesting question to see which gives the better predictions overall. A comparison of the Leuthold and neo-classical models has been made by Ashworth and Ulph (1977b). What they have done is to extend the Leuthold model so that it can be directly tested against the neo-classical model. In the Leuthold model it will be remembered that each spouse's utility is assumed to depend on their leisure and their own consumption. In their extension to the model Ashworth and Ulph let each spouse's utility depend on their joint consumption, their own leisure, and the leisure of the spouse. Clearly if the utility functions of each spouse were identical this extended Leuthold model would be identical to the neo-classical model. The essence of the authors' procedure is to test that extended Leuthold model against the neo-classical model. The models proved to be significantly different statistically, with the Leuthold model giving the better fit.

Results

There are no Type III household results published to date, which is not surprising given the number of problems to be solved simultaneously. Given the evidence that endogeneity matters, particularly for women, this means that we must wait for more definitive estimates. In choosing a study to report, I have been influenced by the Ashworth and Ulph finding that a Leuthold model is preferable to a neo-classical model, and for that reason report a recent study by Jane Leuthold (1979). Her study is a study of US families using data from the 1970 National Longitude Survey. The model is a Leuthold model as described above. To be eligible the

[2] Some may not behave in the way either predicts, for example because they may behave wholly (or in part) as if their budget constraints were separate.

family had to include a woman aged 30 to 44 and both
husband and wife had to be workers. The latter requirement
avoids the problem of an observed wage rate for non-partici-
pants but as was shown in Chapter 7 may bias the results.

The dependent variable was annual hours which was
measured as usual hours per week times the number of weeks
worked, or seeking work. The net wage of the wife was her
gross wage times one, minus an estimated marginal tax rate.
The husband's wage was found 'by dividing the husband's
annual wage income by his annual hours of work' (Leuthold
(1979), p. 152). This procedure was required 'because of data
limitations'. While it is not totally clear it seems probable
that annual hours and the net wage were calculated as in the
case of women.

Leuthold recognizes the potential endogeneity of the marginal tax rate (but not of the overtime premium) and says the
problem is circumvented '*by assuming* that for most families
income falls within tax brackets rather than between them'
(p. 153—emphasis added). The problem with this approach is
that the answer is a question of fact not assumption.

Because the error term for husband and wife are likely to
be correlated, as for example variables such as family back-
ground and political preferences are omitted, Leuthold used a
generalized least squares estimate, which should reduce the
resulting bias.

Leuthold's results are reproduced in Table 8.1. It can be
seen that the own wage coefficient is positive for women and
negative or approximately zero for men. This is consistent
with the results of most earlier work—but it can be seen that
property income term is significantly positive for white men.
It is also interesting to note that the effect of children is, in
general, to decrease the wife's labour supply while increasing
that of the husband.

There are a formidable number of problems that have to
be solved simultaneously even with individual models. All
these problems still have to be solved with household models,
plus the additional complications discussed in this chapter.
There is fairly clear evidence from individual models that
endogeneity is important especially for women. This means
quite a large number of linear segments of budget constraints

Table 8.1 *Seemingly unrelated least squares estimation of hours. Equations for working couples, 1970*

Characteristic	White		Black	
	Wives	Husbands	Wives	Husbands
Constant	1428·96[a]	2273·78[a]	947·22[a]	2016·62[a]
	(5·60)	(18·20)	(2·22)	(11·81)
Own disposable wage	54·30[a]	−137·87[a]	117·64[a]	30·78
	(2·17)	(10·54)	(2·65)	(·85)
Spouse's disposable wage	−33·05[a]	−81·94[a]	41·91	−4·90
	(2·43)	(3·50)	(1·02)	(·13)
After-tax property income	·006	·029[a]	·020	·022
	(·74)	(3·63)	(1·06)	(1·36)
Age	7·67	−27·76	6·72	−26·88
	(1·53)	(1·63)	(·79)	(1·12)
Education	11·94	39·05[a]	31·20[a]	14·09
	(1·33)	(6·12)	(2·35)	(1·58)
Children less than 1	−385·17	50·26	683·60[b]	293·59
	(·93)	(1·28)	(1·71)	(·85)
Children 1–2 years	−480·23[a]	19·40	−78·48	228·00[b]
	(3·42)	(·15)	(·56)	(1·88)
Children 3–5 years	−152·11[a]	28·91	−149·04	−65·29
	(2·48)	(·50)	(1·54)	(·79)
Children 6–13 years	−75·48[a]	−2·39	32·92	−37·76[b]
	(4·03)	(·14)	(1·22)	(1·68)
Children 14–17 years	−2·48	57·27[a]	−35·36	−46·54
	(·10)	(2·49)	(·95)	(1·44)
Health	13·52	—	−95·00[a]	—
	(·49)		(2·01)	
Homeowner	−60·48	83·77[b]	81·50	1·30
	(1·13)	(1·66)	(1·10)	(·02)
Unemployment rate	−14·40	−8·72	9·41	−3·98
	(1·55)	(·99)	(·61)	(·30)
R^2	·079	·164	·158	·062
d.f.	940	941	286	287

Note: Absolute value of t-ratio in parenthesis.
a. Tests significantly different from zero at the .95 confidence level.
b. Tests significantly different from zero at the .90 confidence level.
Source: Leuthold (1979)

for each worker with some of the kinks being convex to the origin and some concave. Clearly the number of such segments will increase as allowance is made for overtime premiums, second jobs, multiple tax rates and means-tested social security systems. When two workers are considered, budget constraints become multi-faceted surfaces rather than piece-wise linear. Thus it is hard to escape the conclusion that there is a great deal of work still to be done!

9

SUMMARY AND POLICY IMPLICATIONS

A great deal has been learned, both in methodical and in substantive terms, about the effects of the tax-transfer system on labour supply. Methodologically we are a long way from the idea that a simple application of the model outlined in Chapter 1 will tell us what we need to know about labour supply. These methodological issues are important. The methodological advances that have been made have highlighted the importance of the common sense view that high quality data is fundamental.[1]

There are *no* studies of labour supply that are not open to serious objection on at least one important ground. Therefore the most intellectually-defensible position is that after a decade of effort we can say very little about labour supply elasticities. This position is a comfortable one for the academic economist in that it absolves him from the responsibility for decisions taken on the basis of his findings. Nevertheless the policy-maker may justifiably want to know what is the best evidence available.

While there are exceptions, based on respectable work, to every one of the following 'stylized facts' they would seem to be supported by current evidence.[2] (1) Women tend to respond more than men to changes in their budget constraints. (2) The responsiveness of both men and women in later, more sophisticated studies (for example, Type III studies) tends to be higher than in less sophisticated studies. (3) The own substitution elasticity is positive as predicted by the theory. (4) The income elasticity is negative confirming that leisure is a normal good. (5) For men the price elasticity is low and negative, perhaps 0.0 to -0.4. (6) For women price elasticity is positive and higher, perhaps 0.8 to 2.0 or 3.0.

[1] Econometric techniques can, to an extent, compensate for data deficiencies; for example, by correcting for truncation bias.

[2] These stylized facts are *in general* consistent with the evidence from the small selection of studies reported in this volume, but also take into account other studies not explicitly referred to.

Policy Implications

Even if we were totally confident that we knew the price, income, and substitution elasticities it would not be easy to work out the policy implications of, for example, a change in income tax rates.

One of the reasons for this is that changes in tax rates will affect the demand for labour as well as the supply of labour.[3] Another problem is that even if one is ignoring the effects on labour demand there may well be a revenue requirement. This might be met by reducing tax rates for some income groups while tax rates for other groups are increased. The design of tax systems to give the best tax rate and the best structure of tax rates is the subject matter of optimum income taxation.[4] Another possible way of meeting a revenue constraint would be to increase certain taxes while cutting others. The reduction in income tax in the UK in 1979, while increasing VAT, is an example, but clearly many other combinations are possible. Each possibility has both theoretical and practical difficulties. For example, Atkinson and Stern (1979) have examined the switch from income tax to VAT using a model in which individuals decide both their labour supply and their commodity demands, given the after-tax prices of commodities and the net return to work effort. While their theoretical structure is a major advance the data they used—the UK Family Expenditure Survey—is so deficient on the labour supply side that their estimates must be treated very cautiously.

Effects of income tax changes

The previous paragraphs have narrowed the problem considerably by sweeping various difficulties under the carpet. What is left is to look at the effects of particular changes in direct taxes and transfers on the supply of labour, ignoring macro-economic effects, general equilibrium effects, and

---

[3] A brief introduction to the incorporation of labour supply effects in a Keynesian model is given in the appendix to Chapter 13 of Brown and Jackson (1978).

[4] For an introduction, see Chapter 19 of Brown and Jackson (1978).

assuming away problems caused by a revenue requirement. We start with the effects of changes in income taxes.

It is easy to fall into the trap of thinking very loosely along the following lines: 'We know from elementary economic theory that a change in income tax is like a price effect: that is to say if the rate of income tax is raised there is an income effect that increases work and a substitution effect that decreases work. The sign of the price effect is indeterminate theoretically but may be estimated empirically. If we know the sign of the price effect from empirical work we can predict the directions of change of hours of labour supply and if we know the price elasticity we can predict the magnitude as well. Thus if the price effect is negative an increase in taxes will lower the net wage and induce the representative man to work harder. Therefore there is no limit to the amount by which we can raise taxes both for redistributive purposes and in order to finance additional expenditure on goods and services.' This would be a useful 'spot the fallacies'-type examination question.[5] Most of the difficulty with the argument stems from two interrelated difficulties: (1) the tax system is progressive and (2) budget constraints are non-linear.

Many of the reasons why this argument is fallacious were discussed in Chapter 2. It was shown in that chapter that a cut in income taxes could shift the supply curve *either* in the direction of *more* work (if the exemption level is raised) *or* in the direction of *less* work (if the tax rate is cut). It was also shown in that chapter that quite substantial changes in tax rates may have no effect on people at kinks in their budget constraints, but that people at kinks in their budget constraints will be affected if the kink shifts. For this reason an increase in exemptions may *increase* the labour supply of those working up to the tax threshold and simultaneously decrease the labour supply of tax payers.

Glaister, McGlone and Ulph (1979) have shown that for an individual near the exemption level the effects of a change in the rate of income tax may be more closely approximated

---

[5] The redistributive part of the argument is essentially part of the optimum tax problem.

by the substitution elasticity than by the price elasticity.
The argument is illustrated in Fig. 9.1 where it is assumed

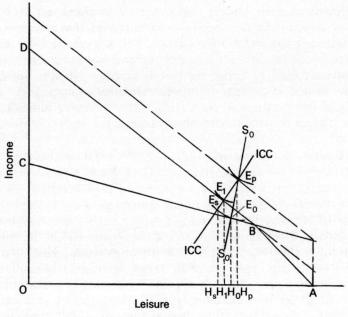

FIG. 9.1.

that a cut in the basic rate of tax changes the budget constraint from ABC to ABD. The effect is to cause the individual to move from E_0 to E_1, that is, to *increase* hours of
work from AH_0 to AH_1. Had the effect been estimated using
the price elasticity it would have been predicted that the
individual would move from E_0 to E_p, that is, he *decreases*
hours of work from AH_0 to AH_p. If the prediction was made
on the basis of the substitution elasticity the predicted move
would have been from E_0 to E_s: an *increase* in hours from
AH_0 to AH_s. It can be seen that the substitution elasticity will
predict too large an increase in hours. (Very near B there
would be very little error in the predictions.) However, the
substitution elasticity predicts correctly an increase in hours
while the price elasticity incorrectly predicts a fall in hours.

It should now be clear that we need to know (1) labour
supply elasticities, (2) the precise tax change under considera-

tion, and (3) details of the distribution of individuals relative to their budget constraints. Without this information we cannot predict whether individuals will move from one segment of their budget constraint to another, and even if they stay on the same segment we have seen that it is easy to mispredict the direction of change. This is a complex exercise that would be difficult to carry out without using the model and data used to make the labour supply estimates. Ideally one should make labour supply estimates using a Type III model (see Chapter 5) then recalculate, for every individual, the budget constraint after the change in tax under consideration.

Glaister, McGlone and Ulph (1979) have done this type of exercise on the Stirling data set. They found a negative, but very small, price elasticity for men and their results confirm the theoretical possibility noted above that a cut in the basic rate of tax may increase labour supply with a negative price elasticity. They found that an increase (decrease) in the basic rate of tax by 5 percentage points (for example, from 30 per cent to 35 per cent) would decrease (increase) labour hours supplied by just over 3 per cent. While this information is probably the best available it should be regarded as illustrative of the method rather than as forming a firm prediction of the effects of tax changes. There are a number of reasons for this but perhaps the most important are (1) that the Stirling data is restricted to weekly-paid employees, and (2) only the effects of the income tax system are considered, that is, the transfer system is not included. The significance of this omission should be clearer in the next section.

The policy implications of the 1979 Budget: an approximation

It has been argued that there are no fully accurate estimates of labour supply elasticities and it seems unlikely that any will be available for several years.[6] Even when reliable estimates are available complex simulations will be required to

---

[6] It seems unlikely that accurate estimates can be made on any existing data sets so that time will be required to collect new data sets.

predict the policy implications accurately. This section suggests a method for approximating the effects of tax changes on men and illustrates the method with the 1979 UK income tax changes.[7] This provides a test of the Chancellor's assertion about the 'keystone' of his strategy which was 'to cut income tax at all levels' because 'this is the only way we can restore incentives and make it worthwhile to work'.

It was argued in Chapter 2 that increases in the exemption level for income taxes will shift supply curves in the direction of less work for people remaining in the same tax band (see Fig. 2.3 on p. 11). If the price elasticity is zero (as it is drawn in the figure) this is the only effect of the tax change. A cut in the basic rate of tax shifts the supply curve in the direction of more work (see Fig. 2.4) and this is again the only effect if the price elasticity is zero (for people in the same tax band). The diagrammatic exposition of the theory becomes more complex with multiple tax rates, but the basic principles are unaltered. Changes in tax allowances, tax rates, and tax bands will change either the intercept of a linearized budget constraint or the slope of that constraint or both. If the price elasticity was zero, changes in the slope of the budget constraint would not affect labour supply. In this circumstance it is possible to predict whether people would wish to work more or less from changes in the intercept (if leisure is a normal good).

The evidence presented in this book suggests that price elasticity for men is a small negative number. If, as a first approximation, price elasticity is taken as zero, we can use the parameters of the tax system to indicate how tax changes are likely to effect incentives at various income levels. The effect of a particular tax change on labour supply can be predicted from the effect it has on the intercept of the linearized budget constraint. If the intercept rises due to the tax change (as in the case of raising the exemption level) there will be an income effect reducing labour supply, while if the intercept falls (as it does when the basic rate is cut)

---

[7] This section considers the total changes in income tax enacted in the Budget. In part these changes were necessary to compensate for inflation. The proposed method could be used to calculate separately the nominal and real changes.

the income effect will increase labour supply.

If overtime premiums and both social security payments and benefits are ignored, the intercept for any tax band can be calculated using the formula:[8]

$$I^i = I^{i-1} + (t^i - t^{i-1})\, y^{p-1}$$

where I^i = intercept, i^{th} bracket

t^i = tax rate, i^{th} bracket

y' = gross income, top i^{th} bracket.

The Tables 9.1 and 9.2 show the intercepts for the 1978-79 and 1979-80 UK tax schedules for single men and married couples with just the husband working, where there are no exemptions other than the single and married person's allowance. The final column predicts whether labour supply will increase or decrease at various income levels. Basic-rate taxpayers should be almost unaffected by the changes because the increase in the intercept associated with the higher allowances is almost exactly offset by the decrease due to the lower basic rate (which reduces the value to taxpayers of the entire allowance). As most taxpayers pay tax at the basic rate this suggests that the income tax changes will not increase the incentive to work for the great majority of taxpayers. No clear prediction emerges for those whose incomes fall below the basic rate band, but those with higher incomes should work more. However, the evidence on labour supply elasticities does not refer to high income people, so this effect is particularly speculative. These predictions offer little support[9] to the view that the 1979 tax changes would increase the incentive to work at all income levels. This could have been achieved by cutting the basic rate even more, instead of raising allowances, but this would have increased income inequality.[10]

---

[8] Brown, Levin and Ulph (1977).

[9] If allowance is made for the possibility that supply curves are slightly backward bending, the support becomes even less. The slight increase in the intercept for basic rate taxpayers who are married further weakens the support.

[10] At least before supply effects are considered.

Table 9.1 *The effects of the income tax changes on the labour supply of a single man*

Income (£)	Tax Rate (%)		Intercept		Labour supply
	1978/79	1979/80	1978/79	1979/80	
0- 985	0	0	0	0	same
986- 1165	25	0	246	0	more
1166- 1735	25	25	246	291	less
1736- 1915	33	25	385	291	more
1916- 8985	33	30	385	387	same
8986- 9985	40	30	1014	387	more
9986-10985	45	30	1513	387	more
10986-11165	50	30	2063	387	more
11166-11985	50	40	2063	1504	more
11986-13165	55	40	2662	1504	more
13166-13485	55	45	2662	2162	more
13486-14985	60	45	3336	2162	more
14986-16165	65	45	4085	2162	more
16166-16985	65	50	4085	2970	more
16986-19485	70	50	4936	2970	more
19486-21165	75	50	5909	2970	more
21166-24985	75	55	5909	4028	more
24986-26165	83	55	7908	4028	more
26166+	83	60	7908	5337	more

Table 9.2 *The effects of the income tax changes on the labour supply of a married man with no children*

Income (£)	Tax Rate (%)		Intercept		Labour supply
	1978/79	1979/80	1978/79	1979/80	
0- 1535	0	0	0	0	same
1536- 1815	25	0	384	0	more
1816- 2285	25	25	384	454	less
2286- 2565	33	25	567	454	more
2566- 9535	33	30	567	582	same/ less
9536-10535	40	30	1234	582	more
10536-11535	45	30	1761	582	more
11536-11815	50	30	2338	582	more
11816-12535	50	40	2338	1764	more
12536-13815	55	40	2964	1764	more
13816-14035	55	45	2964	2454	more
14036-15535	60	45	3666	2454	more
15536-16815	65	45	4443	2454	more
16816-17535	65	50	4443	3295	more
17536-20035	70	50	5320	3295	more
20036-21815	75	50	6321	3295	more
21816-25535	75	55	6321	4386	more
25536-26815	83	55	8364	4386	more
26816+	83	60	8364	5727	more

There are several reasons why these predictions must be regarded as approximations. Where a change in work is predicted, there is no indication of the amount;[11] and also the total change in work could not be estimated without knowing the number of individuals in each income band. Overtime premiums, the social security system and other taxes and allowances are ignored. The results are particularly speculative for those with high incomes, and the method cannot be applied to women, since evidence suggests that their labour supply has a relatively large positive elasticity. The complexities of household decision-making are ignored. The measure at best estimates changes in labour supply but not changes in welfare.

Negative Income Taxes and Means-tested Benefits

The purpose of this section is to discuss briefly the difficulties in drawing policy conclusions from negative income tax programmes and means-tested benefits. Negative income taxes (NITs) pay a cash sum to persons or households that have income below a specified level. This sum is reduced as income rises towards this level. Means-tested benefits (MTBs) provide benefits frequently, but not always, in kind (for example, free school meals, reduced rents) to persons or households whose incomes fall below the level specified for that benefit. NITs and MTBs have certain common features: (1) they raise the net incomes of poor households; (2) as households raise their own incomes (for example, by working more), some, or all, of this benefit is lost. The rate at which the benefit is lost is thus the implicit tax rate on the NIT or MTB. There is in fact very little fresh that needs to be said here about the policy implications of labour supply elasticity that has not already been said above. The problem of kinks in budget constraints continues. Once again people may be located at concave kinks, and may also shift to a different segment of their budget constraint in

[11] For people remaining on the same segment of their budget constraint, estimates could be made by applying empirically-estimated income elasticities to the changes in intercept, but this technique cannot cope with people who move to a different segment of their budget constraint.

response to policy changes. If anything these problems may become more acute because budget constraints can become exceedingly complex if several NIT and/or MTB programmes interact with each other and with the income tax system. This raises in a particularly glaring form the problem of people's perception of their budget constraints. If budget constraints are particularly complex, is it reasonable to assume that low income people (who may have had little education) fully understand these constraints? The answer to this question is probably no. While Rosen (1976) has made an attempt to discover whether there is a misconception effect, this would appear to be an area in which much work remains to be done.

Most studies of NITs and MTBs (including all the NIT experiments) have used special samples deliberately selected to be unrepresentative of the general population. This means that at best these samples can only estimate the labour supply effects on households in the population from which the sample is drawn. Thus we may be told that the effect of a particular programme may be to decrease hours by H, reduce earnings by $, increase disposable income by $Y, all for a cost to the government of $Z billions. The $Z billions obviously has to be found from somewhere. If, for example, it were raised by increasing income tax this would have effects on the labour supply, incomes etc. of persons both outside and, possibly, inside the group for whom the MTBs and NITs were designed.

Conclusions

It is clear that our knowledge of the effects of taxation on labour supply has increased very considerably in the last decade. It should perhaps not surprise us that one of the main things that has been learned is that the problem is considerably more complex than was realized at the outset. Thus while there is a growing consensus about the results there remains a substantial area of disagreement. The policy implications of the studies with the lowest elasticities are substantially different from those with the highest elasticities.

LIST OF REFERENCES

Ashworth, J. and Ulph, D. T. (1977a). Estimating Labour Supply with Piecewise Linear Budget Constraints. University of Stirling, Mimeo. (1977b) 'On the structure of family labour supply decisions'. University of Stirling, mimeo.

Atkinson, A. B. and Stern, N. H. (1979). On labour supply and commodity demands. (mimeo). Paper presented to the NBER–SSRC Conference on Econometric Studies in Public Finance.

Barlow, R., Brazer, H. E. and Morgan, J. N. (1966). *Economic Behaviour of the Affluent.* Washington: The Brookings Institution.

Break, G. F. (1957). Income Taxes and Incentives to Work : An Empirical Study. *American Economic Review,* vol. 47.

Brown, C. V. (1968). Misconceptions about Income Tax and Incentives, *Scottish Journal of Political Economy,* vol. 15.
(1977). Survey of the Effects of Taxation on Labour Supply of Low Income Groups, in IFS, *Fiscal Policy and Labour Supply.* London

Brown, C. V. and Jackson, P. M. (1978). *Public Sector Economics.* Oxford: Martin Robertson.

Brown, C. V. and Levin, E. (1974). The Effects of Income Taxation on Overtime: The Results of a National Survey, *Economic Journal,* vol. 34.

Brown, C. V., Levin, E. and Ulph, D. T. (1974), On Taxation and Labour Supply, University of Stirling discussion paper in *Economics,* no. 30.
(1976). Estimates of Labour Hours Supplied by Married Male Workers in Great Britain. *Scottish Journal of Political Economy,* vol. 23.
(1977). 'Inflation, Taxation and Income Distribution, in V. Halberstadt, and A. Culyer (eds.) *Public Economics and Human Resources.* Paris: Editions Cujas.

Burtless, G. and Hausman, J. (1978). The Effect of Taxation on Labor Supply- Evaluating the Gary Negative Income Tax Experiment, *Journal of Political Economy,* vol. 86.

Cain, G. G. and Watts, H. W. (eds.) (1973). *Income Maintenance and Labor Supply.* Chicago: Markham.

Cogan, J. G. (1978). *Negative Income Taxation and Labour Supply: New Evidence from the New Jersey-Pennsylvania Experiment.* Santa Monica, The Rand Corporation.

Dickinson, J. G. (1975). The Estimation of Income-Leisure Structures for Prime Age Married Males. Doctoral dissertation, University of Michigan.

Fields, D. B. and Stanbury, W. T. (1971). Income Taxes and Incentives to Work: Some Additional Empirical Evidence, *American Economic*

Review, vol. 61.

Godfrey, L. (1975). *Theoretical and Empirical Aspects of the Effects of Taxation on the Supply of Labour*. Paris: OECD.

Glaister, K. E., McGlone, A. and Ulph, D. T. (1979). Labour supply responses to tax changes—a simulation exercise for the UK. Paper presented to the NBER–SSRC Concerence on Econometric Studies in Public Finance (mimeo).

Greenhalgh, C. (1979). Participation and Hours of Work for Married Women in Great Britain. University of Southampton discussion paper, no. 7905.

Gronau, R. (1973). The Effect of Children on the Housewife's Value of Time, *Journal of Political Economy*, Supplement.

Hall, R. E. (1973). Wages, Incomes and Hours of Work in the US Labor Force. Chapter 3 in Cain and Watts (1973).
(1975). Effects of the Experimental Negative Income Tax on Labor Supply, in J. A. Pechman and P. M. Timpane, *Work Incentives and Income Guarantees: The New Jersey Income Tax Experiment*. Washington: The Brookings Institution.

Haveman, R. H. and Watts, H. W. (1977). Social Experimentation as Policy Research: A Review of Negative Income Tax Experiments, in V. Halberstadt and A. K. Culyer (eds.), *Public Economics and Human Resources*, Paris, Editions Cujas.

Heckman, J. J. (1974). Shadow Prices, Market Wages and Labor Supply. *Econometrica*, 42, 4.

Holland, D. H. (1977). The Effect of Taxation on Incentives in Higher Income Groups. in *Fiscal Policy and Labour Supply*, Institute for Fiscal Studies.

Keeley, M. C., Robins, P. K., Spiegelman, R. G. and West, R. W. (1977) The Labour Supply Effects of Alternative Negative Income Tax Programs: Evidence from the Seattle and Denver Income Maintenance Experiments. Part I: The Labour Supply Response Function Centre for the Study of Welfare Policy, Stanford Research Institute, Research memo 38.

Keeley, M. C., Robins, P. K., Spiegelman, R. G. and West, R. W. (1978) The Estimation of Labour Supply Models Using Experimental Data, *American Economic Review*, vol. 68.

Kehrer, K. C. (1977). The Gary Income Maintenance Experiment: Summary of Initial Findings. Research Paper, Indiana University.

Killingsworth, M. R. (1973). Neo-Classical Labour Supply Models : A Survey of Recent Literature on Determinants of Labor Supply at the Micro Level. (mimeo) Fisk University, Nashville, Tenn.
(1976). Must a Negative Income Tax Reduce Labor Supply? A Study of the Family's Allocation of Time, *Journal of Human Resources*, vol. 11.

Kosters, M. (1966). Income and Substitution Effects in a Family Labor Supply Model. Report No. P.3339. Santa Monica: The Rand Corporation.
(1969). Effects of an Income Tax on Labor Supply, in A. C.

Harberger and M. J. Bailey (eds.), *The Taxation of Income from Capital.* Washington: The Brookings Institution.

Leuthold, J. H. (1968). An Empirical Study of Formula Income Transfers and the Work Decision of the Poor, *Journal of Human Resources*, vol. 3.

(1979). Taxes and the Two-Earner Family: Impact on the Work Decision, *Public Finance Quarterly*, vol. 17.

Levin, E., Saunders, P. J., and Ulph, D. T. (1975). Individual Labour Supply Under Weekly Incentive System : A Theoretical and Empirical Analysis. University of Stirling discussion paper in *Economics* no. 35.

Masters, S. and Garfinkel, I. (1977). *Estimating the Labour Supply Effects of Income-Maintenance Alternatives.* London: Academic Press.

McGlone, A. and Ruffell, R. J. (1978). Preferences and the Labour Supply of Married Women. University of Stirling discussion paper in Economics, no. 62.

Rees, A. and Watts, H. W. (1975). An Overview of the Labor Supply Results. In J. A. Pechman and P. M. Timpane, *Work Incentives and Income Guarantees: The New Jersey Income Tax Experiment.* Washington: The Brookings Institution.

Rosen, H. (1976). Tax Illusion and the Labor Supply of Married Women, *Review of Economics and Statistics*, vol. 58.

(1978) The Measurement of Excess Burden with Explicit Utility Functions, *Journal of Political Economy*, vol. 86.

Royal Commission on the Taxation of Profits and Income, *Second Report.* Cmnd 9105, Appendix 1. London: HMSO, 1954.

Ruffell, R. J. (1979) Direct Estimation of Labour Supply Functions with Piecewise Linear Budget Constraints. University of Stirling discussion paper in Economics, no. 77.

Tinbergen, J. (1977). Public Economics and Human Resources in Historical Perspective. In V. Halberstadt and A. J. Culyer (eds.), *Public Economics and Human Resources.* Paris: Editions Cujas.

Wales, T. J. and Woodland, A. D. (1976). Estimation of Household Utility Functions and Labor Supply Responses, *International Economic Review*, vol. 17.

(1977). Estimation of the Allocation of Time for Work, Leisure and Housework. *Econometrica*, vol. 45.

(1979). Labour Supply and Progressive Taxes. *Review of Economic Studies*, vol. 46.

Watts, H. W. and Horner, D. (1977). 'Labour Supply Response of Husbands', in H. W. Watts and A. Rees, *The New Jersey Income Maintenance Experiment*, vol. 2: *Labour Supply Responses.* New York: Academic Press.

INDEX

Ashworth, J., 67, 69–72, 102, 105
Atkinson, A. B., 109

Barlow, R., 40, 41
Brazer, H. E., 40, 41
Break, G. F., 37, 40, 41
Brown, C. V., 30, 34–5, 36, 41–2, 54, 60–7, 69, 70, 76, 114
budget constraints, econometric problems of, 17–20; kinks in, 15–17; multi-segmented, 15
Burtless, G., 67, 83, 88

Cain, G. G., 48–50
capital gains, 28
Cogan, J. F., 79–80

Dickinson, J. G., 54, 64–7

endogeneity bias, 20, 55–7, 58, 65, 67, 71, 95, 97–8, 99, 101, 102, 105
exemption level, 10

Fields, D. B., 37–40, 42
family income supplement (F.I.S.), 27

Garfinkel, I., 46–56
generalized C.E.S. utility function, 71
Glaister, K. E., 110, 112
Godfrey, L., 45
Greenhalgh, C., 97–9
Gronau, R., 91

Hall, R. E., 48, 57–8, 77, 79–80
Hausman, J., 67, 83, 88
Haveman, R. H., 77
Heckman, J. J., 91–2, 94
Holland, D. H., 39, 41, 43
Horner, F., 76, 78

identification problem, 30
income effect, definition of, 4
income, imputed, 28; non-employment, 1, 3, 8, 26–9, 48, 51, 52, 54, 57, 95, 97; other, 27–9
income maintenance experiments, Gary, 81–8; New Jersey, 75–80, 89–90; Rural, 80–1; Seattle and Denver, 88–9
income maintenance programme, 12–3, 21, see also negative income taxes
indirect utility function, 69
interview studies, high income 35–41. low income, 33–5

Jackson, P. M., 30

Keeley, M. C., 88–9
Kehrer, K. C., 84–7
Killingsworth, M. R., 98, 104
Kosters, M., 45, 73

labour supply, theory of, 1–2, 26
Leuthold, J. H., 104, 105–7
Levin, E., 24, 34–5, 36, 41–2, 54, 60–7, 69, 70, 115

Masters, S., 46–56
McGlone, A., 99, 101, 110, 112
measurement problems, data sets, 29; identification, 30; misconceptions, 30; non-employment income, 26–9; questionnaire data, 31; sample selection, 21–4; wage rate, 29; work effort, 24–6
models, family-budget constraint-family utility, 104; Leuthold, 104–5; male chauvinist, 103; neo-classical, 104
moonlighting (second jobs), 14–15
Morgan, J. N., 40

National Longitude Survey (1970), 105
negative income tax (N.I.T.) experiments, see income maintenance experiments

overtime premia, 8–10

policy implications, 109
price effect, definition of, 4

questionnaire data, 31–2

rebate, rate, 27; rent, 27
Rees, A., 77
regression, measurement error in, 17; random error in, 17; reverse income taxation, 12
Robins, P. K., 89–90
Rosen, H., 30, 107, 118
Royal Commission on Taxation of Benefits and Income, 33
Ruffell, R. J., 99, 101–2

sample selection, 21–4
Saunders, P. J., 24
second jobs, see moonlighting
social dividends, 12
Spiegelman, R. G., 89–90
Stamp, Josiah, 31